Dynamics of Rural Development in Delhi

DYNAMICS OF RURAL DEVELOPMENT IN DELHI

SUBHASH ANAND
NETRANANDA SAHU
AJAY KUMAR

RESEARCH INDIA PRESS
New Delhi (INDIA)

ISBN : 978-81-89131-97-5

Price : ₹ 1500/-

First Edition: 2017
Reprint: 2026

Published by :
RESEARCH INDIA PRESS
E-6/34, Sangam Vihar
New Delhi-110062
Phone: 011-26047013, (M) 9818085794
E-mail: researchindiapress@yahoo.co.in

Typesetting by
G. R. Sharma
9968281826

CONTENTS

PREFACE

Rural Development has been receiving increasing attention of Governments across the world. The development of country depends upon development of villages. In contemporary India, the pure categories of "rural" and "urban" community can hardly be found. The rural villages of Delhi are different from rural villages of other states of country. Rural development is not a time bound process, it is continuous effort which requires long time planning and for which certain bold assumptions have to be made. Rural development involves raising the socio-economic status of the rural population on a sustainable basis through optimum utilisation of local resources both natural and human.

Increased participation of people in the rural development process, decentralisation of planning, greater access to credit and inputs go a long way in providing the rural people with better, prospects for economic development. Improvement in health, education, safe drinking water supply, sanitation and housing coupled with attitudinal changes also facilitate their social development. In the area of rural Delhi, Government has implemented numerous programmes, policies and schemes since 1951 for the upliftment of rural masses but even today many villages are not in good conditions. Hence there is an urgent need for an in depth analysis of the impact of rural development programmes, dealing with the change in socio-economic conditions before and after the benefits of programme, change in people's perception and attitude, the level of socio-economic inequality and casteism, people's participation and awareness and the extent of benefit derived from the programmes by the beneficiaries. In order to provide answer of above questions this study has been conducted.

This book has been divided into six chapters. Each chapter is having comprehensive analysis with numerous tables and figures. This volume will be helpful and useful for researchers, planners, social scientists, academicians of various disciplines. We express our sincere thanks and gratitude to Dr. R. B. Singh, Head, Department of Geography, University of Delhi, Delhi and Dr. S. K. Kundra, Principal, Swami Shraddhanand College, University of Delhi for their continue help and support. We are highly thankful to Research India Press, New Delhi and Mr. Ganga Ram Sharma for brining out this volume.

Delhi

Subhash Anand
Netrananda Sahu
Ajay Kumar

Chapter–1

Introduction

India is primarily rural in character. Without development of villages India cannot progress. In the context of India, development means mostly rural development as its two third population live in rural areas. Rural areas contribute significantly to the development of the country in terms of food, raw material, manpower, and market for industrial product and earning foreign exchange through export of agricultural commodities. There is hardly any village without a thin layer of urbanism and similarly hardly any urban center without any thing of ruralism.

Mahatma Gandhi had a better understanding of rural development. He expressed his view in the following lines. "I have believed and repeated many times that India is to be found not in its few cities but in its 7,00,000 villages. I would say that if the villages perish, India will perish too", (Dhillon, 1991).

Mahatma Gandhi and Mao Zedong, who differed radically in both philosophy as well as strategy, shared a common vision of rural development. Both leaders felt that the real answer of the problem of poverty in their countries basically lay in the self reliance, self-government and a high degree of self-sufficiency of the villages, were the goals of their rural development strategy. Both these two leaders clearly feel that their countries because of the diversities of topography, climate, culture and traditions could not ruled from the capital alone. Both stressed in socialownership of the means of production, the role of mass participation and need for the leadership to identify with people.In contemporary political analysis, rural development deals with formulation and implementation of programmes and policies.

Rural development is not an exclusive subject but a blend of both social sciences like economics, sociology, geography, political science, demography, psychology, management and technical disciplines like agriculture, engineering, science and technology etc. Policies and programmes of rural areas, problems and difficulties encountered in their implementation, approaches and strategies adopted by thousands of organisations and individual, the overall impact in all aspects of life and strengthening the base of the rural economy and the nature and level of people's participation form the core of rural development subject matter.

Development of rural economy and the improvement of the village life are chief concern of different scholars of various disciplines. Therefore, it is biggest challenge before the nation. As a matter of fact that till now the urban Delhi has drawn attention of many scholars of associated fields individually as well as organisational level, but the rural Delhi has not given due attention. Actually, it is rural part of the state thathas been affected physically by the legal annexation ofmany villages into urban area. Thus, the rural Delhi should have drawnattention. Now, Delhi occupies first position in urbanisation in the country and has 10.07 per cent rural population of the total population, whichis more than the total population of Arunachal Pradesh. The rural villages of Delhi are not like the rural villages of other parts of country. In Delhi, all rural villages are connected with pucca road and stand electrified. Development in all aspects of life of masses of rural Delhi has taken place due to the benefits of various rural development programmes.

In the pre-independence days rural development was primarily a task of voluntary organisations set up by eminent personalities.

Rabinderanath Tagore's scheme of Rural Reconstruction, the Martandam Experience by Spencer Hatch, The Gurgeon Experiment by E.L. Brayne, the Rural Reconstruction Programme in Baroda, Indian Village's Upliftments Scheme were pioneering ventures in this direction. These schemes were mostly individual initiatives implemented on a limited scale isolated, uneven and discontinuous (Gandhi, 1936). Right from the beginning of planning period, several socio-economic programmes have been designed and attempted by the government to transform the rural scene. Community Development Programme (CDP) and Panchayti Raj system were introduced in 1952 and 1959 respectively to bring and all round socio-economic development of the villages with the willing co-operation and participation of the villagers. Under the Community Development Programme, Alipur block was first development block and has been a showpiece for visitors to Delhi. Later on, other rural development programmes and schemes have been launched and implemented for upliftment and to reduce the gap between rich and poor persons of rural Delhi. Keeping in the mind the significance and economic condition of agriculturallabourers, late Prime Minister Smt. Indira Gandhi launched a 20 Point Programme. This programme shows a better result in improving socio- - economic status of beneficiaries.

Concept of Rural Development

Literally, the concept of rural development has two components: Rural and Development in which rural denotes an area which is characterized by non-urban style of life, occupational structure, social organisation and settlement pattern whereas development means qualitative as well as quantitative socio-economic changes, not only relative but subjective change. Therefore, rural areas are described, as under developed or backward as per capita rural income is low in rural area as compared to that urban area. World Bank defined, "rural development as a strategy to improve the economic and social life of a specific group of people, the rural poor, small scale farmers, tenants and landless." (World Bank, 1975). Agriculture development no doubt constitutes the core but not of rural development. Concept of rural development is much larger than the agriculture development.

The rural development, popularly now known as Integrated Rural Development, requires high technology, administrative hierarchies and co-ordination at various levels for aiming at a comprehensive development pertaining to all aspects of rural economy.

Winnick introduced the concept of "place prosperity and people prosperity". The people prosperity means aid to certain people (such as the unemployed, the poor and the under-privileged, the minorities) and the former means aid to selected place, (like rural, under developed areas, old industrial regions). In a sense, the place prosperity approach implies concern for inter-regional or other dimensions of spatial equity which may contribute towards solving the problems arising from the inequitable distribution of personal income and resultant welfare effect of place prosperity" is a reasonable substitute for proper prosperity, it follows that maximizing specified policy variables within a geographically defined areas becomes also most equivalent to maximizing the welfare of the target population within that area" (Harry, 1978).

Rural Development is a comprehensive programme of activities which includes agricultural growth, development of village industries, development of housing for the poor, planning for public health, education, development of rural transport and communication and child care etc. Out of these aspects, each one requires urban support in terms of goods and services. Modern agriculture inputs like chemical fertilizer, pesticide, high yielding variety seeds, tractors, pump sets and mechanical tools etc. required for agricultural development have to be supplied by the urban sector, so, there is interdependency between these two sectors.

The Gandhi's concept of Rural Development was not that of more economic prosperity for a few at the cost of many; it was about the participation of the entire population in the production as well as consumption unto the least of all. He was always fond of the concept of Gram Swarajya and Gram Vikas and strongly advocated the establishment of a village set up based on his doctrine. The task of rural development implies both economic betterment of the people and effective social transformation necessary for socio-economic infrastructure that is conducive to the multifaceted rural development programmes.

In a nutshell, rural development may be viewed as a programme intended for all round desired development in each component of rural life of all sections of society. Ankar Desmond (1973) views that "strategies, policies, programmes for development of rural areas with the ultimate aim of achieving a fuller utilization of available physical and human resources, and thus higher incomes and better living condition for the rural population as a whole, particularly the rural poor and effective participation of the latter in the development process."

Objectives of Rural Development

The key issues clustering over the whole spectrum of the rural transformation both in the realm of theory and policy making virtually rest on the ability of planners to minimize the persistent poverty, acute unemployment, vast illiteracy and deep-rooted diseases from the rural areas and also to maximize the growing demands of the basic needs of the rural population for improving their living standard thereby making the process of their development more vibrant and self-sustaining. World Bank and other international agencies and institutions did place the main emphasis on increasing production, raising productivity, increasing employment and mobilizing what land, labour and capital were available. But there was also recognition that poverty and inequalities had to be reduced.

To fulfill the objective of rural development the basic needs of the rural population could be divided in two categories; first the individual of family needs such as nutritional food, potable water supply, domestic fuel, shelter etc. and secondly the community needs such as electric power, transport facilities, telecommunication, education, health care and recreational facilities etc.

According to Michal Todaro (1956)the objectives of rural development are:

1. Improvement in level of living standard which includes employment, education health, nutrition, housing and variety of social services.
2. Decreasing inequality in the distribution of rural incomes and in rural-urban balance incomes and economic opportunities.
3. The capacity of the rural sector to sustain and accelerate the pace of these improvements.

Therefore, main objectives of rural development are:

1. Full utilization of available human and physical resources.
2. Development of all sectors of rural economy.
3. To provide basic needs to all rural masses.
4. To bring improvement in the socio-economic conditions with special emphasis on rural poor.
5. Decreasing inequality in the rural income and wealth.
6. To break the cycle of dependency of depressed group.
7. To accelerate the development rate.
8. Effective participation of masses in all developmental activities.
9. Make rural area more and more productive and less vulnerable to natural hazards, poverty.

Science and Technology for Rural Development

For successful implementation of rural development programmes, it is important to provide vital science and technology inputs during the successive stages of implementation of such programmes. For development, change is the key and the primary driving force for such a change is technology. Thus, technology can be effectively utilized to foster high quality development in order to generate prosperity in the rural areas. In 1938, Netaji said, "Agriculture will have to be put on a scientific basis with a view to increasing the yield from the land". An experiment was made in Etawah in 1948 to see the possibility of rural areas through application of science and technology. The main objectives of the programme were scientific agriculture; animal husbandry and to set up small scale industries for new tools.Late Smt. Indira Gandhi emphasized the development of technology in rural areas to reduce the drudgery of rural women.

With the launch of the First Earth Resource Technology Satellite (ERTS-1) by U.S.A. in July 1972 a new vista had opened up for natural resources data collection from space platform. In the current state-of-art remote sensing technology, it is now possible to have a ground resolution capability of 5.8 meters and the improvements in sensor technology have led to higher discrimination capability viz; crop discrimination for enabling a pre-harvest crop production estimation, periodic monitoring of changes in land use patterns. With continuedimprovements in image processing techniques, satellite remote sensing technology has reached the status of routine utilization in the management of natural resource of earth (Chaturvedi, 1998).

The utility of Geographic Information System (GIS) to the end user is not only to access the natural resource data in spatial mode, but also to undertake socio-economic status evaluation in the dynamics of demographic context. Apart from assessing the mutual inter activity of the various natural resources and evaluating the likely consequences of the rural development programmes in the socio-economic, it is easy to accurately monitor the spatial impact of rural development programmes and the technology provides timely data for mid-course corrections, where necessary. Such a management practice would lead to better and more successful implementation of rural development programmes.

In India, especially in rural areas technology has not been utilized for the development activities to the desiredextent. While a number of technologies have been developed and field-tested, they have not been transferred effectively to the rural areas. In the field of education, health, agriculture, rural energy, food processing, construction technology can be utilized for improving the efficiency of produce goods. Drinking water remains a big problem is rural areas and quality beingpoor due to iron content, salination, high bacterial contents etc. such drinking water leads to disease. Bacterial treatment is available. Health is also another important area of concern due to increasing birth rate, high infant mortality rate and emerging new diseases. Efficient energy technique is the need of hour. In the food processing sector about 7 to 10 per cent of our food grains are spoiled due to lack of post harvest technologies. For controlling the land degradation, technology can be transferred and wasteland can be minimized.It will be possible to take investigate decision at the lowest level of decision making on a firmed up and accurate integrated location specific data base for the rural areas.

The spatial distribution of the population of men and women when co-related with the distribution of natural resources would help in deciding the modality of exploitation of the natural resources so as to over-come the discrimination between gender classes. The GIS has the requisite capability to provide timely understanding of the different elements of natural resources and socio-economic and demographic information and thereby helps in preparing multiple action plans for taking effective investmentdecisions. Therefore, it can be said that technique of remote sensing and GIS provides a cost effective real time assessment for decision making in regard to planning and programmes for the rural areas.

With the population expansion in both rural and urban area the analysis with respect to the carrying capacity of land based on science and technology inputs, is essential for sustainable economic growth with adverse consequence on the eco system. New techniques would have to be followed to achieve the objective of evaluating the carrying capacity.

Research Problem

The villagers, due to nearness to towns and cities, communication and transport, imitate the culture of city people but may remain rural owing to the environment. Delhi ranks first in terms of urban population.According to 1991 census rural population of Delhi was 10.07 per cent, which in 2011 is just 2.5 per cent. Decennial growth rate of rural population was 8 and 11.0 percent in 1971-81 and 1981-91 respectively, which during 2001-2011 was just 2.5 per centRural people change their life style gradually and adopt a quasi-urban way of life.

The success of rural development programmes depends on the benefit, which can derive to the most needy segment of rural based society and to the identification of areas where help is most essential. Any deviation from this fundamental principle may lead to the total or partial failure of the development process. Any development programme for the poor when it gets implemented tends to deviate from the poor and gravitate towards the richer section of society.

A number of efforts have been made so far by the Government, whichhave shown the result. Rapid urbanisation process in Delhi created socio-economic and environmental problems for the people of rural area and also due to increasing the level of urbanisation and industrilisation, occupational pattern and people's attitude is changing. Studies and survey shows that the desired goals of rural development are not achieved satisfactiorly mainly because of the some shortcomings of the programmes and lack of people's participation, no co-ordination among various agencies and departments.

Despite of implementation of various rural development programmes and schemes, a required growth rate has not taken place and still many villages are suffering from lack of infrastructure facilities. Most of the skilled and efficient craftsmen and artisans are not in better condition and lack of employment opportunity compel to younger unemployed person falling in crimes.

One of the most important manifestations of the socio-economic structure of rural society is the helpless dependence of the poor on rich and landlord. Although the rural development programmes try to help the poor in various ways, but do not attach on this dependence. Most of the programmes do not have holistic approach and failed to fulfill the needs of rural masses.

One of the main reasons for failure of programmes is lack of people's participation. In spite of numerous developmental efforts, masses of rural Delhi are facing the problem of scarcity of felt needs and basicinfrastructure facilities. Hence, there is urgent need for an in-depth analysis of impact of rural development programmes that how were the socio-economic conditions before and after the benefits of programme, how is people's perception and attitude changing, the level of socio--economic inequality and casteism, people's participation and awareness and what was extent of benefit derived from the programmes by the beneficiaries. In order to provide answers of above questions thisstudy has been conducted.

Review of Literature

In this investigation many related studies were consulted. The studies of various dimensions and problems of rural areas helped much in the formulation of research problem and its methodology. There are number of studies on assessment, evaluation and impact of different Rural Development Programmes but there is lack of literature on rural development programmes of Delhi.

Mathai (1971) identified key communicators among rural women and suggested their crucial role in motivating that rural women leaders are more progressive and innovative and have the unique ability of convincing rural women about developmental programmes. Puri (1974) studied the Najafgarh block and told that animal-related tasks were pre-dominantly wife-central and was mostly performed and also the decisions were also taken by them.

Singh (1977) had measured the tele-viewingbehaviour on the basis of the frequencies of programme's viewing and ways of the viewing the programmes. The changes brought about by the respondent after having viewed the programme and the critical ability of the viewers to have preference towards various aspects of farm telecast.

Alexander (1980) has done the study on the impact of economic development on different aspects of social life and he argued that lack of knowledge to use local resources and exploit economic opportunities considerably limited. It was noted that respondent of Abhnapur were more socio-economically advanced than the respondent of the Bhilaigarh. Majority of the respondents believed that unclean people should not allowed to draw water from village wells, not the Harijan people.

Upreti and Upreti (1981) in their study of inter-caste relationship in Kumau, found that Brahmins and Harijans are politically homogenous group as they all voted to one party. It is opposite the general assumption that Harijans are vote bank of a particular political party. Singh (1982) reported that big farmers derived more benefit from the banks than small and medium farmers and agricultural labourers.

Madan and Madan (1983) have mentioned that the success of Community Development Programme in

Mohana block was confined to only a few items and few agriculturists. Ahuja and Bhargave (1984) reported that 23 per cent of all beneficiaries under IRDP crossedthe poverty line after getting assistance.

Krishnan (1984) described that the selection of beneficiary families was not proper as only 16 out of 80 samples households were really eligible for assistance under IRDP. Sekha (1984) has done study on impact of operation flood I & II on rural development. He concluded that the dairy movement has helped to break down barriers between castes. To climb out of abyss of rural poverty one certainly need much more than alleviation one need self reliance, self determination and dignity of labour which can be gained through a co-operative and concerted effort. Hirway (1984) reported that 55-75 per cent of thebeneficiaries were non-poor who dominated among the other beneficiaries of the programme. Malyadri (1985) argued that programme had a strong impact on the income distribution of the beneficiaries and their employment creation also increased after receiving the financial assistance under IRDP. Planning Evaluation Organisation (1985) conducted a study on IRDP and reported that about 88 per cent of the selected households increased their income and 64 per cent felt that their overall status in the village society had been elevated. Singh (1985) has argued that programmes can succeed with the people's participation and this participation should be from the beginning of programmes. Mohan Sundram (1988) described that the co-ordination among developmental agencies was very much lacking not only at the implementation level but also at the stage of undertaking follow-up measures. Thangamuthu and ManimiKalai (1989) found in their survey on generating of employment for women through DWCRA that the beneficiaries had crossed the poverty line with additional income of Rs. 285 to Rs. 460.Usha (1990) reviewed the experience of rural development programmes particularly IRDP, NREP and RLEGP.

Prasad (1991) has mentioned some drawback of rural development programme like lack of measurable parameters, which make goals and targets more manageable and over commitments of the bureaucracy as to the delivery of services and developmental activities. Dhillon (1991) evaluated the IRDP in Punjab with critical appraisal of ineligible beneficiaries and inadequate assistance. Ramachandran (1991) statedthat the initial impact of the city is seen on agricultural land use in the villages.

The city offers a market for product that the village is in a position to supply such as milk, vegetables, fruits etc. The daily interaction between city and village in itself generates a process of social and economic transformation of the village community.

Training Orientation and Research Centre (1993) has conducted a study survey and reported that there is lack of infrastructures facilities and felt needs in many villages of rural Delhi. It makes a list of assets in rural Delhi. Koche (1994) has observed that the rural development programmes gave more emphasis on economic aspects and they have neglected essential social aspects. These programmes have tended to give rise to social tension and conflicts.

Sexena (1994) found that generative rural towns could benefit more to those villages, which are situated either quite close or well connected with good link roads and having the adequate facility and goods-cum-passengers transport services. He further reported that during1971-81 due to impact of generative rural town, size of agricultural holdings of the respondents increased.

Gardam (1995) has mentioned that land reform, poverty eradicate programme does not bring any real change in living standard of the poorest and he further reported that reports of eating snails as food by tribal, selling of babies, Arabs marrying minor Indian girl, child labourers in hazardous and inhumane environment jobs are very common. These are basically eventualities of wrongly defined definition of poverty. He told that Indian do not feel the need to change of definition of poverty.

Diwakar and Qureshi (1995) outlined the utilization of compensation money after land acquisition in rural Delhi in 1961-85. Sen (1996) focuses on how transformation can occur in rural development through self help by the people.Chandra (1996) has mentioned that poor implementation of developmental programme should not be taken as an excuse by the government as well international bodies to withdraw their support. Panda (1996) has found that rural unemployment and population growth, farm productivity and health care could be some of the important priority areas for technology transfer and then could be devise region, specific programmes because districts vary in all aspects. Gupta (1998) has done study on Technology Transfer in the context of Orissa Tribal Development Project (OTDP) he found that "on farming training" has significantl effect on rural developmet.

Purpose of Study

The purpose of the present research study is to find out and analyse the impact of rural development programmes on socio-economic conditions. The study covers the programmes which have implemented since 1975in study area.

The main objectives of the research study are:

1. To analyse the impact of development programmes on socio-economic conditions of the people particularly poor.
2. To understand the level of participation and awareness of the people.
3. To make suggestions for the improvement of socio-economic conditions of the people.

In order to achieve the above mentioned objectives, the following hypotheses have been formulated.

1. Rural development programmes reduce regional disparities.
2. The benefits of special programmes for the poor are not reaching them as intended.
3. Lack of awareness leads to low level of people's participation in programme.

Study Area

Delhi is largely the part of Indo-Gangetic plains. It lies at an average height of 200 meters above mean sea level. The latitudinal extent of Delhi is between 28° 24' 17" to 28° 53' 00" North and longitudinal extent is from 76° 50' 24" to 77° 20' 37" East. To the northwest and in the south it is bounded by Haryana State, while to the east of it lays the Uttar Pradesh (Figure 1.1).

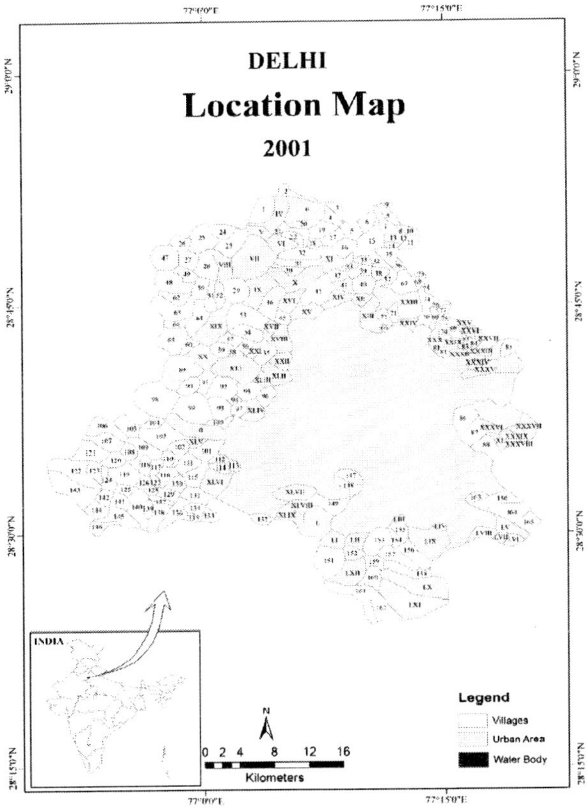

Figure 1.1: Location map of the study area

The study area comprising only the rural part of the National Capital Territory of Delhi covers an area of 782.8 square kilometer. The rural Delhi comprises two tehsils 1. Delhi Tehsil and 2. Mehrauli Tehsil, Both the tehsils together comprises a total of 209 villages and out of this 199 villages are inhabited 134 villages of the inhabited villages belongs to Delhi tehsil and 75 belongs to Mehrauli Tehsil.

Master plan for Delhi divided the rural areas into five development blocks, namely Alipur, Najafgarh, Kanjhawala, Mehrauli and Shahdara. The boundaries adopted for the delimitation of study area are the same as those adopted by the census of India in 1991.

The total rural population of Delhi according to census of 2011 is 4,19,042. It was 9,49,019 in 1991 and 4,18,675 in 1971. Najafgarh block occupies first position in terms of maximum rural population and maximum number of villages, on the other hand Mehrauli block has minimum number of villages.. Scheduled caste population living in the rural area constitutes 23.2 per cent by the total rural population.

In the study area Integrated Rural Development Programme(IRDP),National Rural Employment Programme (NREP), Rural landless EmploymentGuarantee Programme (RLEGP), land Reforms, 20 Point Programme, Training for Rural Youth for Self Employment (TRYSEM), JawaharRozgarYojna (JRY), Development of Women and Children in Rural Areas (DWCRA), Integrated Rural Energy Programme (IREP), Rural Water Supply Programme (RWSP), Integrated Development of Rural Villages (IDRV) etc. are implemented by various agencies and departments. In spite of formulation and implementation of above mentioned programmes many villages are suffering to lack of infrastructure facilities and low status of socio-economic conditions. Decreasing cultivable land, sanitation, encroachment by J.J. colonies and industrial unit, increasing unemployment and pollution etc. are major problems.

Research Methodology

The present research work is aimed to study the impact and changes in socio-economic condition brought by rural development programmes in rural Delhi. The study is based on two types of data sources i.e. primary and secondary data source. The important research techniques administered in the present investigation are mainly framing of the interview and observation schedules for collecting primary information concerning the problem. Official statistics were collected through secondary source. After condensation of all the primary and secondary data their classification and suitable tables were drawn for analysis.The methodology adopted two phases (Table 1.1).

First Phase: Secondary Data Collection

The secondary data have been collected from various agencies, departments, institutions, journals, magazines and census reports etc. The information and data about all rural development programmes were obtained from the Development Department and National Institute of Rural Development, Hyderabad (NIRD). Planning Commission provided relevant data and useful information regarding total amount allocated to rural development sector in each Five-Year Plan for Delhi, Delhi Development Authority (DDA) being responsible for better development of Delhi, helped in supplying the detailed information regarding all developmental efforts. Directorate of Economics and Statistics supplied required dates on socio-economic indicators. The background information pertaining to area, land use pattern, demographic characteristics has been collected from District Census Handbook, Primary Census

Table 1.1
Research Methodology

Data Collection			
Primary Data Sources			*Secondary Data Sources*
Surveyed Village	*Block*	*Selected Benefi-ciaries*	*Organizations*
1. ZindPur	Alipur	20	Development Department
2. Nangli Poona	Alipur	20	National Institute of Rural Development
3. RewlaKhanpur	Najafgarh	20	Delhi Development Authority
4. PundwalaKhurd	Najafgarh	20	Census of India
5. Kanjhawala)	Kanjhawala	20	Planning Commission
6. Qamruddin Nagar	Kanjhawala	20	Central Statistical Organisation
7. Mithapur	Mehrauli	20	Directorate of Economics and Statistics
8. Jonapur	Mehrauli	20	Govt. of NCT of Delhi
9. Gharoli+ Biharipur	Shahdara	20	Reports, Books, Journals, Periodicals
10. Sabhapur	Shahdara	20	Unpublished Materials

Abstract and Gazetteer of Rural Delhi. Reports, articles, research paper published in various magazines and journals and other important documents proved of immense help.

Second Phase: Primary Data Collection

The research study requires primary survey in order to bring people's perception on socio-economic transformation. Filling interview schedule and observation through direct personal contact collected the data and informations from the beneficiaries. The field survey was conducted among those villages, which were benefited by20 Point Programme. This programme was selected for household survey because except from this programme, villagers did not have information of any other rural development programme. Out of total villages, two villages of beneficiaries per block were selected randomly; so total ten benefited villages were chosen. In ten sample rural villages, one is Khanjhawala which is census town according to 1991 census. It was deliberately chosen because around 1976 there was happened an event known, as "Kanjhawala Case" has its own place in history. The ten selected villages for households survey were Zind Pur, Nangli Poona, RewlaKhanpur, PundwalaKhurd, Kanjhawala, Qamruddin Nagar, Meethapur, Jonapur, Sabhapur and Gharoli.

For household survey, forty samples of beneficiaries, under 20 Point Programme per block and total 200 households were selected on random basis. Under this programme, Surplus Gram Sabha land was distributed to the landless low caste families and ex-military servicemen, so, survey was conducted among beneficiaries but in many villages benefit was also given to non-eligible families so they also surveyed where they found. For assessing the list in the socio-economic status of beneficiary, a questionnaire and list of indicators of socio-economic index was prepared This exhaustive interview schedule was divided into five parts contains questions on background information of respondent and his family, second and third parts tries to collect information about socio-economic status index such as caste, occupation, income, education, agriculture land, debt, savings, housing condition, drinking water, source of energy for cooking and animals etc. Fourth part is relatedto the health and last part of the interview schedule contains people's perception, opinion and suggestions.

Therefore, 200 beneficiaries from whole study area were interviewed personally through exhaustive questionnaire. Questions about other rural development programmes were also asked. Participatory Rural Appraisal (PRA) being a popular technique in rural research is also used for getting real observation. After getting the primary and secondary data, their classification and appropriate tables were drawn and statistical diagrams were made.

Data Processing and Analysis

After completion of the field survey, the data was processed. All the entries were thoroughly checked and omission and other problems were rectified. The preliminary dimension of analysis was the background of the respondents and their families. After that their socio-economic data and people's participation and perception analysed. Socio-economic indicators were co-related to each other. The cartographic techniques used are bar graphs and pie diagram etc.

Limitation of the study

The study was carried out with the following limitations.

1. The findings of the study are based on the expressed opinions of the respondents. Although every effort was made to secure accurate information from the respondents, the possibility of a respondent giving biased information cannot be completely ruled out.

2. Study area is very vast so intensive study cannotbe made.
3. A Kanjhawala village was one of the selected villages, for survey, which is not rural village, it is census town according to census of India, 1991.
4. Household survey was done among those who were benefited under 20 Point Programme, so, research study in mainly based on impact of 20 Point programme on socio – economic conditions of low caste people.

Organisation of the Study

To fulfil the aims and objectives of the research study the entire research work has been divided into six chapters. The first chapter deals to elaborate the introductory aspects to rural development, mentioning the research methodology, research problem and aims and objectives of research study. Second chapter explain with the geographical profile of study area. This chapter is divided into two parts,part A describes the physical aspects and part B deals with human and socio-economic aspects. Third chapter highlighted rural development programmes and schemes of Delhi. Fourth chapteranalysed the impact of programmes. Level of participation and awareness has been discussed in fifth chapter. In the last chapter conclusion and summary has been presented.

References

Anker Desmond, L. W. (1973) "Rural Development Problem and Strategy", International labour Review.

Chaturvedi, R.S. (1998), "Science and Technology inputs in Rural Development Programme", Journal of Rural Development, vol. 17, No. 2.

Dhillon, D.S. (1991) "Integrated Rural Development", Vohra Publication & Distributors, Allahabad.

Gandhiji (1936), Harijan, Quoted from Shah, S.M. Rural Development Planning and Reforms, Abhinav Publication, New Delhi.

Harry, W. Richardson. (1978), Regional and Urban Economics,Penguin, p.221.

Todaro, Michael, P. (1956), — Economics of Developing World,Longman Group Ltd. London.

World Bank (1975), Rural Development :Sector Policy Paper, World Bank, Washington.

CHAPTER–2

GEOGRAPHICAL PROFILE OF RURAL DELHI

PART - A
PHYSICAL ENVIRONMENT

Delhi under Different Historical Periods

The name of Delhi seems to have made its appearance for the first time during 1st and 2nd centuries A.D. Ptolemy and Alexanderine marked "Daidala" in his map of India close to Indraprastha and midway between Mathura and Thaneshwar (Delhi Administration, 1976).

Fifteen different cities are believed to have been found at different times on different sites within this perimeter, and each has left behind its cultural and social remains resulting in the Delhi of today, which is an admixture of civilization, tradition, a variety of cultures and social background. The earliest known city of Delhi is Indraprastha, which is associated with the Pandavas. It is said to have been situated on a huge mound on the western bank of the river Yamuna, now occupied by the Purana Qila. In the first century B.C. Raja Dillu is believed to have built another city on the site where Qutab Minar now stands and named it Dilli. The next city was Surajkund, built by a Tomar Rajput Raja Anangpal, in A.D. 1020. Anangpal and his successors, who ruled for about a century, converted the town, into a five-walled city calledLai Kot. The famous iron pillar is associated with this dynasty. The Prithvi Raj Chauhan, the last Hindu ruler of Delhi expanded the city for times. The end of his reign saw the muslim invasion in 1191 and his defeat in the battle of Panipat. Qutab-ud-din Aibek, a slave of the invader, Mohammed Gauri, to whom was entrusted this conquest, took the liberty of proclaiming himself the first Sultan of Delhi and retained the old capital. One of his successors, Ala-ud-din Khilji (1296-1316) built a new city at Siri, about three miles north east of Delhi. A huge tank associated with this city was the Hauz Khas. In 1321, Ghiyas-ud-din Tughlak built another city known as Tughlakabad. His successor Mohamad-bin Tughlak built a new capital city called Jahanpanah at a site between Dilli and Siri. This was the fourth of the seven cities of the Delhi Plains. In 1354, his successor FerozShah, transferred the capital to a new town Ferozabad, about eight miles north of Dilli and two miles north of Indraprastha.

In 1526, after the Killing of the Ibrahim Lodhi, Babar established the Mughal dynasty and his son Humayun began building a new capital at the old site of Indraprastha, which he called Din-e-pannah, but because of his defeat at the hands of Shershah Suri he could not complete the city, which was later completed by the victor. After this, Shahjaha, grandson of Humayun built a new city Shahjahanabad two miles north of Ferozabad.

Delhi was first constituted as a territory in 1803 when General Lake defeated the Marathas in a battle at Patparganj, captured Delhi and brought the Mughal Emperor, Shah Alam under his control. The cityalong with the neighboring territory known as the assigned tract comprising the districts of Hissar, Rohtak, Gurgaon, Delhi and Karnal was placed under the charge of an officer designated as Resident and Chief Commissioner of Delhi. From 1862, the Delhi constituted of three tehsils Sonipat, Ballabhgarh and Delhi. On December 12, 1911 where a Commissioner announced the change of capital from Calcutta to Delhi a separate Province of Delhi came into existence.

Delhi continued to be a centrally administered territory under the provision of the Government of India, Acts of 1919 and 1935 upto January 26, 1950 when Delhi became a part C state under the new constitution. Under the part C states act 1951, Delhi was granted legislative assembly with 48 members and was administered by a regular constituted ministry responsible to the local legislature.

Under the State Reorganization Act 1956, and the seventh constitution amendment act 1956, Delhi was constituted as a Union Territory and the legislative assembly was abolished but in 1993 legislative assembly of 70 members was formed again and third assembly was formed in 1998.

Location

Delhi is lying within a narrow strip of the Indo-Gangetic Plain between 28° 24' 17" to 28° 53' 00" North latitude and 76° 50' 24" to 77° 20' 37" East longitude. The river Yamuna separates from Uttar Pradesh particularly Ghaziabad and Meerut districts in the east. On theother sides the villages border on Sonipat, Rohtak, Gurgaon and Faridabad districts of Haryana (Delhi Administration, 1987).

Physiography

The river Yamuna and the Aravali range dominate the physiography of Delhi, and the plains in between formed by alluvium deposits of recent formation. The Delhi Ridge and its four sections the northern, the central, the south central and the southern constitute the farthest extension of the Aravali range, its spurs meeting the Yamuna at two points, in the north and the east. Ecologically, the ridge acts a barrier between the Thar desert and the plains and slows down the movement of dust and wind from the desert. The ridges of the Aravali range extend right into Delhi proper towards the western side of the city and this has given an undulating character to some parts of Delhi. As the area is a part of watershed of two-river system of India sub-continent one is the Ganga system in the east and another in Indus river system in the west. Bordering the Thar desert of Rajasthan, Delhi tends towards aridity, but being on the verge of the Gangetic plains, rural Delhi is fertile plains. Summers are dry and very hot, but with planned afforestation, natural forests being denuded in the area, the severity of dry summers have become milder, humidity has also increased. The interaction between the different aspects like relief, soil, vegetation and hydrology has made this land system well suited to different types of land uses.

Hilly Relief

The villages of Delhi are situated between the Thar-Aravali barriers, projecting from the south-west and the Himalayan ateliers hanging from the north. Physiographically, the most important feature of the region is the ridge. This relief feature is almost triangular in shape with a wide base in the south and a narrow apex in the north. The ridge of Delhi is the culminating spur of the Mewat branch of the Aravali Hills and enters the Delhi from south extending upto River Yamuna in north. The north most tip of the ridge is visible up to Wazirabad. The ridge is not continuously open now-a days as much of it has been covered by build up area of the city.

The tail end of the last spur of the ridge goes south-wards upto Mehrauli and then turns towards Badarpur and Tughlakabad along the Delhi-Haryana border. The relief has its maximum altitude at Bhati, 318 meters in the south and lowest at Wazirabad 208 meters above sea level in the north. Ridge has a maximum width of 2.5 Kilomater west of Chanakyapuri and minimum with of 50-100 meters at Wazirabad. Apart from the main branches, there are several other spurs of less significance, which give a complexity to the whole system. The rock is highly jointed and it is along these joints that water percolates and removes cementing material. There is found a zone of loose grains along the outer rim of the jointed block of rock due to leaching of cementing material. The loose grains are removed by external agents of surface of the earth, which leads in lowering of spur incumbent weight.

Geologically the out-cropping rocks of area belong to the pre- Cambrian period. These rocks are said to belong to the Alwar series and predominant among them is Delhi/ Alwar quartz, which is made up of compact quartzite, grits and conglomerates with minor clay and limestone beds (Delhi Administration,1976).

The hills are highly dissected due to erosion through centuries and there are many ravines separated by low ridges mostly bare of negative cover. Now, hills and ridge attain maximum an elevation 150 meters above the ground in the whole area.

The only significant lines of drainage in this part are the Bara Pulah Nala and the Tekhand Nadi. The former drains the hilly area lying to the north east of Mehrauli and latter drains the west area of Mehrauli. Sahibi is a river that has its catchment area is Rajasthan and through Haryana it enters Delhi at Dhansa. From Dhansa the course of the river is canalised and linked with the Najafgarh drain.

Plain

The whole plains of Delhi are Gangetic plains and are wide fertile in the north but towards the south they are almost lost in the maze of rocky undulations. It has more or less uniform height (average elevation varying between 650 feet to 750 feet above sea level). The plains of rural Delhi can be divided into four units (i) Khadar (ii) Bangar (iii) Dobar (iv) Kohi.

These four types of soils are suitable for different crops.

Soil	*Crops Suitability*
Khadar areas with enough Moisture	For vegetable of cucurbit type
Bangar areas	Paddy is the most successful crop
Dobar areas	Frequent flooding
Kohi	Depending an availability of irrigation. It suitable for a variety of field crops, vegetables andorchards.

The Khadar

The Khadar is a low-lying stretch land adjoining river Yamuna. According to the origin Khadar and Bangar belong to the same type. The area of recent deposits by the river is called Khadar or new alluvium. This area is flooded during the monsoon season. It comprises Alipur and Palla in the north, trans-yajnuna villages on the east. The river Yamuna enters the Delhi at the an elevation of 216 meters and leaves it at the 192 meters above sea level and has wide sandy beds flanked by high banks. A greater percentage of deposits are found to be of a younger age, which come to occupy a lower level than that of the earlier deposits. Since these plains are liable to inundation very frequently they are considered to be still under the process of formation. The area is proving to floods and soil texture varies from coarse sand to clay with PH value on the alkaline side. The water table is high, facilitating irrigation and hence good cropping.

The Bangar

The area of old alluvium or old deposition called Bangar and has undergone a similar process of formation as the Khadar. The general level of Bangar is higher than that of Khadar and the water table is comparatively lower. Unlike Khader this area of Bangar is free from frequent inundations by the river.

The Bangar zone is characterized by patches of saline effloresce scene and canal irrigation. The Bangar area is the stretch of land to the north-west of river Yamuna and comprises Narela, Bawana and Nangloi tracts. The soil is of silt sand or loam with PH around neutral except in some place.

The Dobar

Dobar is a low-lying and rain-fed area situated to the west of the hilly terrain. Actually, this is a large basin receiving the surface run-off from the hills. In the time of good rainfall an area about 50 square kilometers gets flooded. The Dobar zone has depressions like Najafgarh Jheel. The catchment area of this depression extends over a large area. Apart from Najafgarh Jheel, Dobar zone has some other minor depressions too. The dobar covers the south-western and western tracts adjoining the hilly zone of the south. It comprises Najafgarh- Galipur and Rakrola areas adjacent to Palam village. There are numbers of smaller depressions near the villages, which are used as village ponds.

The Kohi

The Kohi.or Pahri covers the areas of hilly tracts in the south and ridge. This land is found to adjacent of rocky area. Relief map of Delhi shows four major units of physiography.

Drainage System

The river Yamuna entered the Delhi near the Palla village at an altitude of 690 feet above sea level and leaves it near Jaitpur village at an altitude of 650 feet above sea level. The course within Delhi territory measures roughly 51 kilometers with a fall of 18 to 20 inches per 1.6 kilometers. A local watershed west of the River Yamuna, divides the drainage system of the area into two parts (1) eastern and (2) western the eastern portion drains itself into the River Yamuna while the water from the western part flows into the large depression in the Dobar region that is Najafgarh Jheel. There is evidence that the course of Yamuna has changed several times, perhaps always shifting eastwards.

Traces of the old courses and ox-bow lakes lying westward of the present river channel in the northern part of the area of the study. The river Yamuna widens considerably during the rainy season and when flooded it threatens wide areas in the northwest and the east. In the northern part of the area of study, the western Yamuna canal flowing over the crest of the watershed forms the main dividing line between the two drainage systems. To the west, the main outlet is provided by Mungespur drain, which rises in Haryana close to the Delhi. After flowing through the neighbouring areas of Haryana the drain reappearsin Delhi and flow eastwards. It joins Najafgarh canal near Hastsal village. Another drain, named Nangloi drain joins Najafgarh canal near Saiyed village.

The very important drainage channel lying wholly within the Delhi, is the Najafgarh Drain. Originally this drain was cut out from the Najafgarh Jheel in 1838 to provide an outlet for surplus water from the huge Dobar depression into the Yamuna. Flowing through thickly inhabited several villages and raining the urban areas of Delhi in its lower reaches, the drain joins the Yamuna at Wazirabad.

In the southern part of the area of study which is primarily hilly in character, numerous small drains rush down the rough terrain of the Kohi region and drain into the adjoining depressions.

Climate

Climate is the long-term atmospheric character of a specified area. Because of location of Delhi and the prevalence of the air of the continental type during the greater part of the year, climate of Delhi is semi-arid. An extremely dry and hot summer and similarly an extremely cold winter are the main characterstics of the climate. The monsoon winds penetrate upto this area of the country only during the monsoon period from July to September. A year can be divided into four-distinct seasons (i) Winter (ii) Summer (iii) Rainy (iv) Post - Monsoon period.

According to Meteorological Department, Delhi receives an average an annual precipitation of 660.1mm. The rainfall tends to decrease towards northwest and west. Around 3/4 of the total precipitation isassociated with the Monsoon period (IMSO. Only a fraction of the total precipitation is received from westerly depressions during the winter months. The south-west monsoon brings rains to Delhi during monsoon season. The south-east monsoon has a milder impact. The variability of rainfall is found great. The meteorological data reveals that during the 50 years period from 1901-1950 the rainfall in Delhi was highest in 1933 amounting to 232 per cent of the normal and lowest in 1929 amounting only 40 per cent of the normal. Total rainfall in 1995 was 850.9 mm.

January is the coldest month of study area with a mean daily maximum of 21.3° celsius temperature and the mean daily minimum of 7.3° celsius. Winter temperature falling below freezing point under the influence of cold waves is not uncommon.

A change in temperature starts in mid-march and it rises to the maximum by May and June. Delhi sometimes experiences the extremes of heat and the maximum daily temperature as much as 47° celsius is recorded. In the months of April-May hot winds, known as "loo" blow and the weather becomes unpleasant; with onset of monsoon the temperature starts decreasing and humidity increases. April and May are considered the driest months by relative humidity of 30 per cent in the morning and 20 per cent in the afternoon. While from July to September humidity is found highest. For 1996 Delhi as a whole, average temperature was recorded 24.6° celsius.

Urbanization influence the all-climatic parameters,viz temperature,humidity, evaporation, precipitation, radiation, wind speed, water balanceetc. Climate in general determines the energy level of a man in a given combination of climate parameters. Climate influences human health directly through the effect of its vagaries and extremes. A new dimension to the health problem is being added by the rapid destruction of forests and grasslands, soil erosion, silting of natural water drainage system, accumulation of industrial gases in the atmosphere and pollution of the atmosphere and water caused by chemical effluents.

Natural Vegetation

Delhi, which is one of the polluted cities of the world is an example to quote where greenery is essential to protect its severely deteriorating environment. Urbanisation in this capital city has not only denuded most of the wood lands it had put threatens to convert the remaining green areas into a concrete jungle. A land use pattern analysis in 1994 revealed that most of the notified area has been encroached upon by urban uses or is being cultivated.

Forest plays a very important role in maintain a balance in the eco system. Besides, they bestow many benefits to man and their usefulness is not diminished. The study area, which is primarily rural in character, comprises of large tracts of agricultural land. Almost the entire area in the northern and western parts is classified as cropped land. So, there is hardly any natural vegetational cover in this part. The hilly terrain and rocky outcrops in the southern part are barriers for agricultural activities. These patches are either covered by natural vegetation or are under other uses. Generally the vegetation of Delhiis semi-arid, open, scrub forest type and broadly classified under tropical thorny secondary forest. The vendless open fields interspersed with villages having semi circular at once distinguish the landscape of rural Delhi from the urban. Practically, there is no green belt except in abandoned places, religious sites and outskirts fringing the crop fields. The vegetation of Delhi belongs to two-type (1) Hilly area (2) Marshy area. The vegetation of Hilly area is found in south western, southern and southeastern. The vegetation is xerophytes with less varied plant communities having a fewer species. Acacia (Kikar) is found commonly. This type of flora is quite adapted to drought conditions. However, aridity affects the growth of the plants and their size is restricted to bush in most cases. During the monsoon season, sparse and open vegetation cover becomes a quite dense. Marshy depressions, seasonal ponds drainage canals and Yamuna river supports aquatic vegetation. For controlling the floodwater during monsoon,high bunds are constructed along jheel and drainage canals.

The vegetation of these manmade habitats exemplifies the social forestry and comprises fast growing trees such as Acacia, Arabia, Eucalyptus etc. The trees which are found commonly in study area are Albizia lebbek (Siras), Azadirachta (Neem), Dalbergia sissoo (Shisham), F. religiosa (Pipal), F. Virens (Pilkhan) etc. (Delhi Administration,1986).

Most of the land surface is occupied by the agricultural pursuits, and the natural vegetation has been replaced by cultivation.

Forest development is closely linked to climate. Over the years if seems that Delhi climate has been changing rapidly; in particular there has been less of rainfall during the last few years. The reduction in forest cover is bound to affect the climate, which in turn, will have implications for the health of the people. Delhi is already facing a number of problems due to shrinking of forest cover (Figure 2.1 and 2.2).

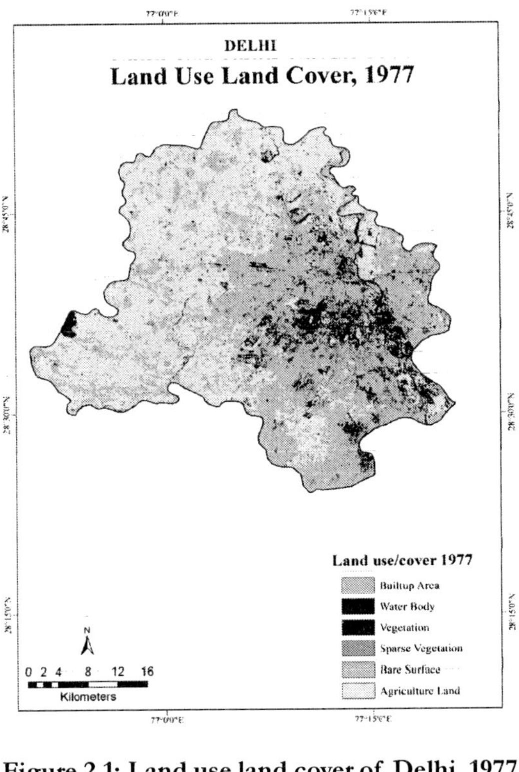

Figure 2.1: Land use land cover of Delhi, 1977

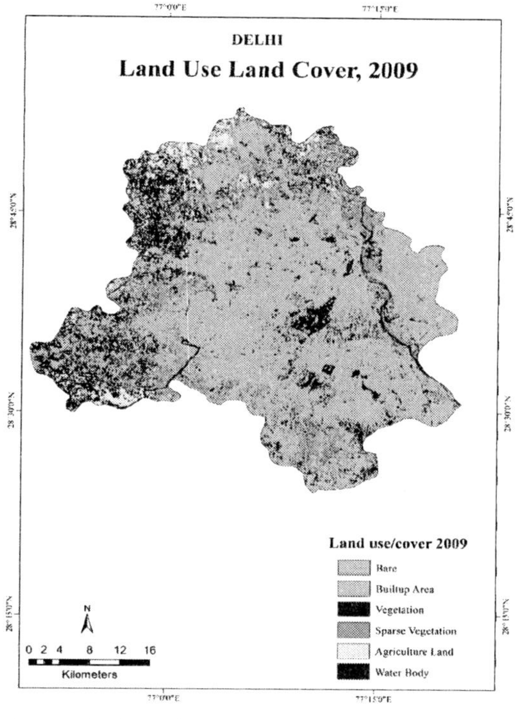

Figure 2.2: Land use land cover of Delhi, 2009

PART - B
HUMAN AND SOCIO-ECONOMIC ASPECTS OF RURAL DELHI

Rural area means the population living in villages and village means any local area whether compact or otherwise recorded village in the revenue record of Delhi state and includes any area which the Chief Commissioner may or special order published in a official gazette declare to be a village.

Earlier there was one tehsil at Delhi and a sub-tehsil at Mehrauli but December 1, 1967 Mehrauli was made a full fledge tehsil under a seperate Tehsildar. Each tehsil is subdivided into field Kanungo circles. Delhi tehsil comprises Delhi, Narela and Najafgarh circles whereas Mehrauli tehsil comprises Mehrauli and Palam circles. Each field Kanango circle is headed by a Naib-Tehsildar under the overall control and supervision of the Tehsildar.

The census of 1891 and 1911 of Delhi was carried out as a part of the Punjab that comprised the tehsils of Delhi, Sonipat and Ballabhgarh with a total area of 1276 square miles. In 1912, a separate Delhiprovince was formed with the area of 1536 square kilometers, after this marginal modification has occurred in the area of Delhi as it was 1484 in 1931 and 1487, 1497, 1484, 1485, 1483 and 1483 square kilometers in 1941, 1951, 1961, 1971, 1981, and 1991 respectively. In 1961 the total rural area was 1157 square kilometer which was 78 per cent of total area. And in 1991 it comes down 797 sq. kilometers which was 53.7 per cent of the total area of Delhi. In 2011 the area decreased to 556 sq. kilometers.

The number of total villages as well as uninhabited or deserted villages has been decreasing. After the partition of country Government acquired many villages to rehabilitate the migrant people from Pakistan. Due to the urbanisation process urban area encroaching the rural villages at fast rate. In the decade of 1961-7118 villages of Delhi were urbanised but in the 1971-81 and 1981-91 the number of villages encroached by urban area were 44 and 15 respectively.

Master plan for Delhi has divided the whole rural area into five blocks i.e. Alipur, Najafgarh, Kanjhawala, Mehrauli and Shahadara. Before 1960, Delhi had three blocks Alipur, Najafgarh and Shahdara. From the area point of view. Najafgarh block is the largest among the exiting five blocks and Alipur has second rank but minimum numbers of villages are in the Mehrauli and Shahdara blocks. Now Kanjhawala and Mehrauli blocks have not any deserted village.

Population

People are an assets if there is balance between the resources and the population. When the resources are few and the number ofpeople is more than region is said to be over populated.Paul Enrich in his book. "Population Bomb" warned that if higher rate of growth is not checked human race would breed itself into catastrophic crisis wherein the limited physical resources of the earth would no longer be able to support the world's overgrowing population.

The human being has its central position in developmental activities. There is a famous saying that "Nau Dilli, Dus Badli and Satt Wazirabad". It means that Delhi, Badli and Wazirabad were ravaged and rebuilt nine, ten and seven times respectively. Badli and Wazirabad suffered repeatedly because of their proximity to the center of power. Delhi being the center of power must have attracted people from far and wide therefore the composition of population of Delhi must have been largely influenced by its geographical location, metropolitan character and political situation (Delhi Administration, 1987). Prabha Chopra in her book, "Delhi: History and places of Interest", mentioned that the population of Delhi stood at two million* in Aurangzeb's time. 0.5 million after the sack of Delhi by Nadir Shah, which further shrank to only 0.1 million in the early years of the present century. When British rule started in Delhi in 1803 the population was estimated 1,50,000 and after the revolt of 1857 this figure was reduced. In 1868, total population was recorded 1,54,417. V.K.R.V. Rao and P.B. Desai in his book told that in 1881 when the first census was done total population of city was 1,73,000. (Rao and Desai, 1960).

Table 2.1
Urban and Rural Population of Delhi

Year	*Total Population*	*Urban Population*	*Rural Population*
1901	405819	208575	197244
1911	413851	232837	181014
1921	488452	304420	184032
1931	636246	447442	188804
1941	917939	695686	222253
1951	1744072	1437134	306938
1961	2658612	2359408	299204
1971	4065698	3647023	418675
1981	6220406	5768200	452206
1991	9420644	8471625	949019
2001	13,850,507	12905780	944727
2011	16,787,941	16,368,899	419,042

Source: Census of India

Table 2.1 reveals that the population of rural Delhi as well as urban Delhi is continue increasing. Since 1901 to 1991 the first time a sharp increase in Rural Delhi's population was recorded during 1941-51 period. The percentage growth in the decade of 1951 was 38 per cent. The reasons for this high growth rate were the partition of the country in 1947 when Delhi received an influx of large number of refugees from Pakistan. Second decade of highest growth rate of rural population was 1981-91. In this decade 109.86 per cent growth rate was estimated owning to shortage of housing facilities and congested or environmental problems in urban area. During 2001-2011 the population of rural Delhi experienced a negative growth of -55.64 per cent. In Urban Delhi, higher rate of growth of population is more a result of a higher immigration rate rather than a higher rate of natural increase. Data on area, density, population variation and sex ratio for urban, rural and Delhi as a whole for 1981, 1991 and 2011 has given in Table 2.2.

Table 2.2
Some Demographic Data on Different Factors

	Area		*(in sq. km.)*
	1981	*1991*	*2011*
Urban Delhi	591.9	685.34	927
Rural Delhi	891	797.66	556
Delhi	1483	1483	1483
	Density (persons per square km)		
Urban Delhi	9745	12361	17658
Rural Delhi	507	1190	754
Delhi	4194	6352	11320
	% Variation of population		
	1971-81	1981-91	2001-011
Urban Delhi	58	47	26.83
Rural Delhi	8	110	-55.64
Delhi	53	51	21.21
Sex Ratio (females per 1000 male persons)			
	1981	1991	2011
Urban Delhi	808	830	868
Rural Delhi	840	807	852
Delhi	810	827	868

Source: Census of India.

The sex ratio (females per 1000 males) of rural Delhi is constantly higher than sex ratio of urban area of Delhi upto 1981 but in 1991 it was lower as it was 807 females per 1000 males while for whole Delhi it was 827, Since 1901 to 1991 sex ratio for rural Delhi is decreasing except in 1931 and 1961. Upto 1981 sex ratio of Delhi as a whole was lower than rural Delhi but in 1991 it was higher. The sex

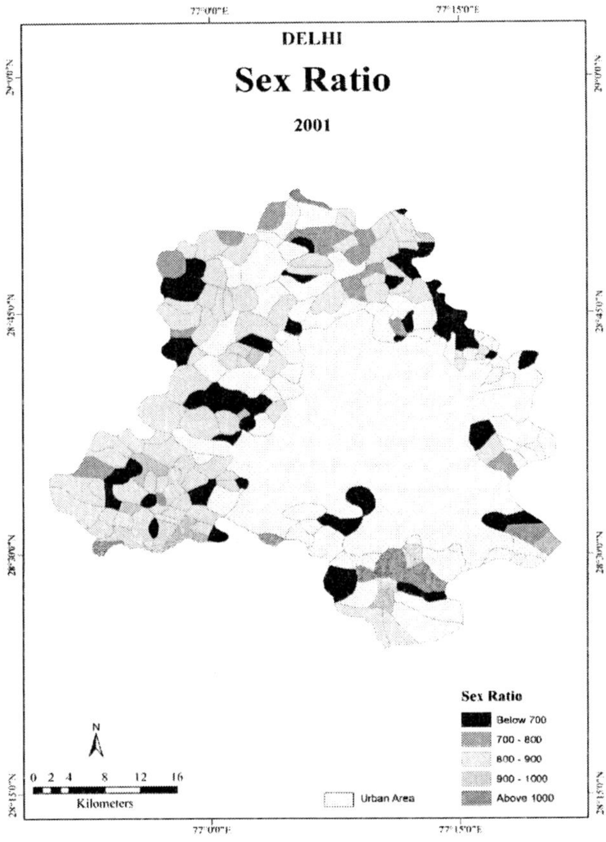

Figure 2.3: Sex Ratio in Rural Delhi, 2001

ratio in rural Delhi increased to 852 females per 1000 males in 2011. Blockwise highest sex ratio is found in Najafgarh and Kanjhawala block and lowest in the Mehrauli.

Population Density

The density of population is an important determinant of economic progress of a region. In the Delhi tehsil the population density is 1293and in Mehrauli tehsil 1169 persons per square kilometer and 57 villages are in the range of 500-1999. According to 1981 census no village was recorded of having population of 10,000 but in 1991 census 21 such villages were found and most of these villages were in Shahdara block (Census of India, 1991). The population density of rural Delhi in 2011 has been recorded to be 754 persons/ sq. kilometer (Table 2.3).

Table 2.3
Density and Sex Ratio of Rural Delhi

Year	*Sex Ratio*	*Density (person per Sq.km)*	*% of Rural Population to total*
1901	916	135	48.6
1911	869	123	43.7
1921	845	140	37.7
1931	860	144	29.7
1941	846	171	24.2
1951	837	243	17.6
1961	847	258	11.3
1971	825	403	10.3
1981	840	514	7.2
1991	807	1189	10.07
2011	852	754	2.50

Source: Census of India

This situation reflects the effects of nearness to the urban core. Even the farthest villages in the Mehrauli tehsil are not more than 20 kilometer far from the outer limits of the urban core, whereas a large number of villages in the Delhi tehsil are more than 15 kilometer away from the city rim. The Mehrauli tehsil's villages are generally preferred for residence by the people who come to Delhi from other parts of thecountry. The density of population of rural Delhi is continue increasing since 1901 as it was only 135 persons per square kilometer in and 243 persons in 1951. In the 1991 it reached upto 1189 persons per square kilometer while it was 514 in 1981 therefore there is highest increase in this decade due to higher rate of immigration.

Difference of population density is not only found between rural and urban area but also within the rural area too. Out of 199 villages, 128 villages have population density of more than 500 persons per square kilometer and 40 are in between 300-500 persons per sq. km. Flood proneness of some parts of the area in the northern and north eastern parts near the city has resulted comparatively lower density of population. The rugged rocky terrain in the south affects the density of population in a similar manner. In spite of productive soil of Dobar Zone, area has lower density due to flood proneness. The area which provide a greater environmental and economic security are comparatively more populations than those parts which suffer from insecurity and poor in resource.

Population data tells that proportion of rural population has been declining's just like the rural area. In 1901 the rural population constituted 48.6 per cent of the total population of Delhi and in 1951 this proportion reduced to 17.5 per cent and in 1981 it was 7.27 per cent. But in 1991 this proportion increased upto 10.07 per cent of the total population of Delhi.

Table 2.4
Growth of Rural Population

Year	*Total Rural Population*	*Male population*	*Female population*	*Shortfall of female population from male population*
1961	299204	161992	137212	24786
1971	418675	229424	189251	40173
1981	452206	249833	202373	47460
1991	949019	525056	423963	101093
2011	419042	226,321	192,721	33600

Source: Census of India.

It was pointed out from Table 2.4 of population of rural Delhi that gap between in total number of male and female is widening as in 1961 male population of rural Delhi constituted 54.1 per cent which increased in 1991 at 55.3 per cent so in 1961 difference was of 24,786 but in the 1991 it became 1,01,093 and in 2011 it decreased to 33,600.

Among the all blocks, maximum per cent of rural populationwas found in Najafgarh which has 27.8 per cent of the total rural Delhi's population and Shahdara occupies second rank with 26.2 per cent but this block has minimum rural area so population density in high. Alipur block has 18.9 per cent rural population in 50 inhabited villages. Out of the total rural villages 86 are in the population range of 2000-4999.

In the area of study the scheduled caste population constitute 23.2 per cent of the total rural population. This per cent is more than nations average per cent and of urban Delhi scheduled caste population. Out of the total 2,07,709 persons, 1,44,924 were in the Delhi tehsil and 62,785 were in Mehrauli tehsil. In 1991 census Buddhistswere also included in the scheduled caste population. Highest number of scheduled caste population were living in the Najafgarh block which has 34.7 per cent and lowest in the Mehrauli which constitute almost half of the Najafgarh block's scheduled caste population. According to Government documents no scheduled tribe has been recognized in the Delhi.

Rural Society

Rural societies are predominantly involved in the production of food, fiber and raw material and have close relationship to the nature and also have the characteristics of homogenous in racial and social relations, so rural communities differ from urban communities in many ways. As the human being to live together different types of human relationship are established. The descendants of a family are united through kinship and thus kinship of the same kin is an important component of social structure. Marriage takes place within a group of relations these groups belongs to an endogamous subcaste or caste. Gradually, many castes and sub-castes came into existence. In spite of presence of the communities from many parts of the country, most of the communities of Delhi are part of the biosocial structure of the population of the north-west and the north. The partition of country brought about a change in the cultural profile of Delhi. After the independence, Delhi came to be dominated by the socio-cultural system of the north west. The refugees introduced a new work ethic, a new dynamism and a new sense of pride. Now a days Delhi is considered as the "Mini India".

As the national capital Delhi has drawn people from all parts of India. At the level of folk perception the migrants are identified as Purabias, (the people from east) Madrase (the people from south) and Paharias (the people from hills).

Social Structure

In Delhi, majority of the communities are Hindus with 75.51 per cent of the total population, followed by Muslims and Sikhs. In the Hindu social system, varna is only a reference category. It is not a functioning unit of social structure, and only refers broadly to the ascribed status of different caste. The three upper levels-the Brahmin, occupy the top place in the hierarchy, followed by Kshatirya, and Vaishya. The Shudra, the fourth level, includes a multiplicity of artisan and occupationally. M.N. Srinivas has defined caste "as a hereditary, endogamous usually localized group having a traditional association with an occupation and particular position in the local hierarchy of caste relations between castes are governed among other things by concept of pollution and purity and generally maximum commonality occur with the caste (Srinivas, 1978). Every person has its own caste by birth and each caste has its own occupation. A "Clean" and "noble" occupation give a caste higher ritual and social status and "unclean" and polluting occupation relegate it to a lower status. The notion of clean and unclean, purity and pollution enter into intra and inter caste behavior and interaction. But things are changing, contemporary reality is gradually drafting away from tradition. In the villages of Delhi, mainly castes are Jat, Gujar, Brahmin, Rajput, Ahir, Bania, Chamar, Jatav,Kashyup and Balmiki etc. Jat forms the largest segment of rural society in Delhi and Jat of south Delhi connects with the Jat ruler of Bharatpur. Most of the villages of Jat and Ahir are in the western part of river Yamuna and Gujar villages are mainly found east and south of this river. Rajput and Chamar villages more or less spread all over the rural Delhi. Although caste dominance is found still in rural Delhi but not like of 20-30 years ago. In village society inter-mixing of the dwellings of Brahmin, Jat and Bania can be seen but not frequent intermixing of Brahmin, Jat and Harijans. There is found sharp cut between upper castes and Harijans. In the central parts of the villages high and middle castes habitation is found and surrounding periphery of this area is allowed to be used by artisans such as barber, black smith and carpenters and others. Outermost area of the village is occupied by the lower castes. In most of the villages Harijans blocks are located either in the southern or western part of the periphery of the settlements.

Mahatma Gandhi gave Harijan term to Dalit, meaning is people of God. During the earlier period the Harijans were allowed to settle only on the eastern and southern margins of the villages so that the drainage and the winds from their localities should not pass through the locality of higher caste residents. The winds blow here generally from north and west direction. The condition was given in view of the fact that most of the Harijans were engaged in skinning the dead animals and making shoes from the leather and the winds and drainage from their locality could spread foul small in the village, if they were allowed to settle in the northern or western parts of the village. Butbecause now almost they had given up this tradition occupation, so inter-mixing of upper caste and lower caste is increasing. Caste and occupation can not now go together.

Although the different social groups lived in almost separate caste quarters but socially unity is found at village level. At present, in villages of Rural Delhi traditional rural social system is losing its tightness and with the time it becoming weaker and weaker. For example many lower caste families are living in close vicinity of the middle and higher caste families. They exchange the goods and domestic material of daily uses and participate in family and social function. However, the caste feeling still prevails among the villagers. Some old age lower caste people reported that about twenty years ago, they were ignored, neglected and suffered by the upper castes but now they were treated as respective persons and upper caste people do not have feeling of exploitation.

The impetus of urbanisaton of rural society brings in various urban values and social change. Traditional importance of caste system in selecting a specific type of occupation by the villagers was weakened and people came out from the traditional cultural. However, lack of facilities, such as transport, education and modern innovative ideas etc. during the early stages created certain problems for the possible innovations. But the gradual expansion of the city, improved transport links with the city, and frequent contacts with the urban population, gave a new direction to the villages and they were forced to make social and cultural change.

The role of women is more significant. She plays the role as backbone of the family. Apart from attending to routine household work of cleaning the house, vessels, fetching of water, cooking and child- rearing, rural women perform innumerable other function in agriculture and related activities. Studies show that a woman works more than a man. Because old generation women and mostly illiterate so they have conservative thinking and they are not ready to adopt innovation and modern life style. Female persons of rural Delhi mainly wear suit- salwar and old age male persons bind the turban on their head.

Hindu people do not marry within a particular area of villages that is called a "Kherra" Although Muslim communities have right to marry anywhere but they follow the custom of Hindu and do not marry in same village. Muslims share many features of the regional culture in which they were located. Rural people marry within their caste but out side of Gotra and practice of Kanyadan and dowry system is found. Arranged marriage is prevailing but rare case of love marriage can be seen.

India's caste system has been much criticized, both at home and abroad yet varna and Jati (caste) name had extraordinary durability and resilience. They appear to survive in some form or other all the assaults on them. But with changing times they have to adapt. Untouchability is based on the concept of pollution and purity that again is attributed to the caste and the occupation of a particular group of people. Masses who considered low in the caste hierarchy because of transmitted pollution and those who dealt with pure object remained at the top ofsocial hierarchy system, (Dube,1966).

Law has abolished untouchability but its practice continues less. Mainly Harijan low caste people suffer to the evil of untouchability. They are discriminate by the upper caste at community and caste level. Several developmental programmes started and assisted the weaker sections in matters of health, education, occupation, sanitation etc. Even so this social evil is still prevalent at lower level. Most of the respondents said that openly higher caste people do not have feeling of untouchability but internally they have. A few told that even today they are suffering to this evil and discriminated in social functions. Actually in rural Delhi the level of untouchability was very high 20-30 years ago but now a days it becoming weaker and younger generation do not believe in principle of untouchability.

Language

Delhi comes in the Hindi heartland region of India. In study area, Hindi is dominant language with marfy dialects. Urdu is the second largest speaking language after Hindi and Punjabi is third. These three languages represent the influence of neighboring states such as Haryana, U.P. and Punjab. From the speaking point of view, rural Delhi can be classified into four groups 1. Dobari 2.Bangru 3.Gujari 4.Braj. Little difference is found in four dialects. The Dobari dialect is spoken in Najafgarh and this is very close to the dialect of Gurgaon district of Haryana. In the north and north western Delhi, Bangru group of Hindi language is spoken and it has great influence of dialect of Sonipat. This dialect has greater sphere of influence and a large part of ruralDelhi speak this dialect. The Gujari dialect is spoken in the eastern Delhi and is akin to the dialect used in Trans-Yamuna region of U.P. Lastly Braj is mainly spoken in the south of rural Delhi and it bears affinity with the dialect of Ballabgarh and Palwal districts of Haryana (Delhi Administration, 1987). Apart from the regional level dialects at village level are also found there. Villages near to urban area follow the speaking style of urban area.

Rural villages has more impact of urbanisation as in each and every aspect a thin layer of urban life style can be seen but with the having non-rural custom they are not ready to give up their rural culture.

Rural Housing

The area of rural Delhi has flat roofs of the houses because of semi arid climate. Generally the entrance to the house is kept on the smaller side of the rectangular. In almost all houses, the courtyard is generally found. The courtyard has mutt uses in different seasons. The corner of the courtyard used cooking, bathing and for cattle space or used as centre of more activities. The house has two main parts one is "Baithek" another is Ghar. The main entrance of house is mostly found through the Baithek. Baithek is used by male persons and guests. Many poor families have one house, which serves as Ghar and Baithek but comparatively richer family have more than one house, used independent for different purposes. Apart from the Ghar and Baithek many of the rural families have another house called Gher. It is used for keeping the cattle during the daytime. Gher is unbuilt spacesurrounded by a boundary wall. Mostly grandfather and grandmother of family lead the last stage of life in Gher.

Table 2.5
Rural Housing (%)

Year	*Pucca*	*Semi Pucca*	*Kutcha*
1981	67.90	26.70	5.40
1991	86.63	5.87	7.50
2008	98.20	1.50	0.30

Source: National Institute of Rural Development.

Data shows that during 1981-91 the per cent of Pucca house and Kutcha houses raised but in the case of semi-pucca houses the per centage declined considerably in Rural Delhi and in 1991 the housing shortage was 9000 houses.

Table 2.6
Families having Different Size of Houses in Rural Delhi (%)

Block	*Small size below 3 rooms*	*Medium size 4-6 rooms*	*Large size above 6 rooms*
Alipur	25.0	52.5	22.5
Najafgarh	40.0	40.0	20.0
Kanjhawala	22.5	67.5	10.0
Mehrauli	22.5	60.0	17.5
Shahadra	32.5	52.5	15.0
Rural Delhi	28.5	54.5	17

Source: Personal survey.

Table 2.6 reveals that in rural Delhi maximum houses are medium size which have the number of rooms 4-6 followed by small size houses but large size house are only 17 per cent of total surveyed houses. Alipur block has more per centage of large size houses than the small size house Delhi. In the category of medium size house, maximum were found is Kanjawala block followed by Mehrauli. Najafgarh block has highest per centage of small size house but lowest were found in Kanjhawala and Mehrauli. No of rooms are close related to the size of families. The number and dimensions of the rooms in the house are a function of the economic status of the family as the personal survey reveals that out of total surveyed families 42.5 per cent have the double storey house.

Literacy and Fuel

Census data reveals that literary rate for rural Delhi is 81.86 per cent (Census of India, 2011) and highest is found in the block of Najafgarh and lowest in Mehrauli. Male and female literacy is the highest in Najafgarh. The male and female literary rate for rural Delhi is higher than nation's average. Delhi tehsil has higher literacy rate rather then the Mehrauli tehsil. Along with literacy rate total number of literate is more in Delhi tehsil villages (Figure 2.3).

Table 2.7
Distribution of Rural Household using Different Types of Fuels for Cooking (%)

Fuel types	*Per centage*
Kerosene	39.43
Cow Dung Cake	24.08
Cooking Gas	17.95
Wood	16.00
Charcoal	1.00
Coal	0.53
Bio-Gas	0.44
Electricity	0.13
Other	0.55

Source: National Institute of Rural Development.

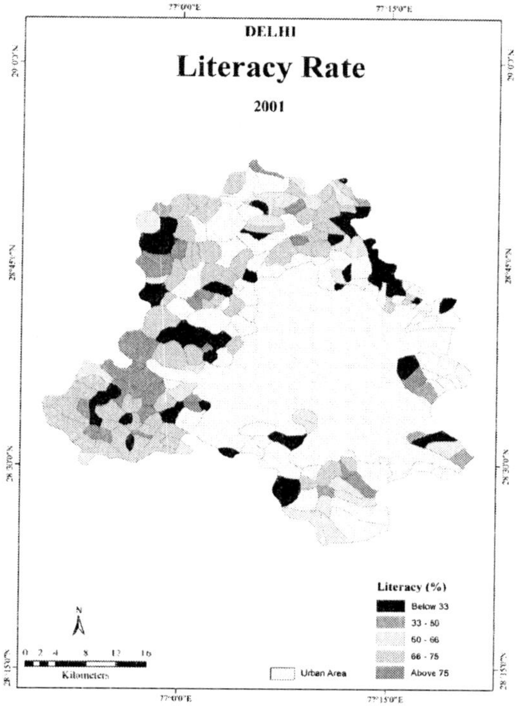

Figure 2.4 Literacy level in Rural Delhi, 2001

In Rural Delhi area, maximum households use kerosene, cowdung cake and cooking LPG gas for cooking purpose but the per centage of cow dung cake is decreasing and use of cooking gas is increasing with time. This LPG gas is better than cow dung cake from health and environment point of view.

EconomicAspects

The essence of development is not in "providing" but in "promoting" the rural sector. Rural development involves raising the socio-economic status of the rural population on a sustainable basis through optimum utilization of local resources, both natural and human. A feature with serious implication is the rapidly increasing population; it consumesaway an increasing share of the surplus, leaving meager amounts for capital formation. According to Meier the definition that would gain wide approval is one that defines economic development as "the process whereby the real per capita income increase over a long period of time subject to the stipulation that the number below on "absolute poverty line" does not increases and that the distribution of income does not become more unequal (Gerald, 1976).

Delhi has the highest per capita income in the country. It accounts for the highest per capita investment in development of the infra-structure and other aspects of development. In the 1980-81 at current prices the per capita income of Delhi was Rs. 2900/- and Rs. 11,657 in 1990-91 (Delhi Administration, 1995). The state income of Delhi has been growing since 1994-95 at an average rate of 8.7 per cent as compared to 6.6 per cent growth rate at the national level. In 1995-96 the per capita income increased to Rs, 18,814/- as against Rs. 9,321- at the national level. The per capita expenditure in 1991 was Rs. 491.73. Out of the total expenditure 6^.15 per cent spent on the food and 39.85 per cent on non food. In other words, rural people of Delhi spent Rs. 295.77 per capita on the food and Rs. 195.96 on the non food items. In the food items, a big amount goes to milk and milk products.

According to National Sample Survey 1991, 70.83 per cent of households of rural areas belong to monthly per capita expenditure of Rs. 385 and above. The N.S.S. also reveals that about 11.9 per cent people of total population of whole Delhi are below poverty line. Out ofwhich 5.6 per cent population belongs to rural areas. For measuring the poverty line criteria has been selected on the basis of monthly per capita expenditure of Rs. 181.50 in rural areas by the Planning Commission at 1991-92 prices. The implementation of various poverty alleviation programmes has resulted in some reduction in the level of poverty rate in rural area. Government has fixed minimum wage for labour Rupees 68.50 paisa per day for both female and male in 1998. Which is the highest in the all states of country.

Villages of Delhi, which have co-existed with the sprawling urban settlement, still retain a great deal of rural tradition. But farmhouses of the rich people are mushrooming bringing urban culture of different kind to the rural people. Rapid urbanisation has relegated agriculture to a secondary position. The pattern of utilization of land in Delhi has changed significantly and now the land is bring used for commercial purposes instead of agriculture purpose.

Table 2.8
Utilizations of Land in Delhi(in hectare)

Year	*Net sown Area*	*Total cropped Area*
1960	87406	113,482
1970	80510	116,585
1980	58551	87,595
1991	48357	76,239

Source: Agriculture Census.

Table 2.8 and 2.9 shows that during last three decades net sown area and total cropped area has decreased significantly. The number of agriculture land holdings belonging to less than one hectare of land increased from 15,000 to 26,000 during 1985-86 to 1990-91, therefore their average size of holding has gone down from 0.43 hectare to 0.29 hectare. However in the case of medium class i.e. 2-4 hectares the number of holdings and their average size of holding remain the same during the above mentioned time period but the number of holdings belongings to the size class of 10 hectare and above have gone down from 505 to 431 and their average size of holdings decreased from 14 hectares to 12 hectares.

Table 2.9
Distribution of Operational holding and their Size in Delhi

Size Class	*No. of Holding*		*Average size of Holding (in ha)*	
	1985	*1990*	*1985*	*1990*
Below 1.0	14933	25811	0.43	0.29
1.0 — 2.0	5283	7565	1.45	1.08
2.0 — 4.0	4970	4933	2.87	2.41
4.0 — 10.0	3591	3201	5.94	5.14
10.0 — above	505	431	14.20	12.22
All Categories	29,282	41,941	1.94	1.17

Source: Agriculture Census.

The agricultural census reveals that out of 41941 operational holdings in Delhi during 1990, about 58.5 per cent of the total were individual holdings while 41.2 per cent were joint holdings and the remaining 0.3 per cent were institutional holdings.

The total irrigated area of Delhi was 56,565 hectares in 1980- 81 and 65,638 hectares in 1995-96 but unirrigated area was 8129 hectares in 1995-96.

Total agricultural production was recorded 1,30,158 metric tons in 1995-96. Out of total agricultural production maximum comes from food crops such as Wheat, Paddy, Bajra and Jawar etc

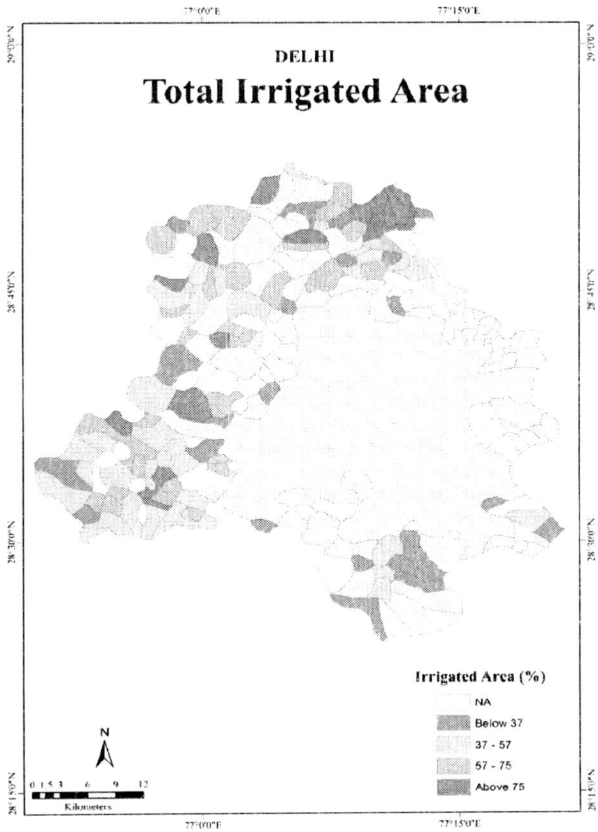

Figure 2.5: Irrigated area in Rural Delhi, 2001

Work Force

Total work force in rural Delhi is 29.1 per cent of which 28.7 per cent are main worker and 0.4 per cent are marginal worker. Census of India 1991, defined a main worker as those who had worked for more than six months treated as

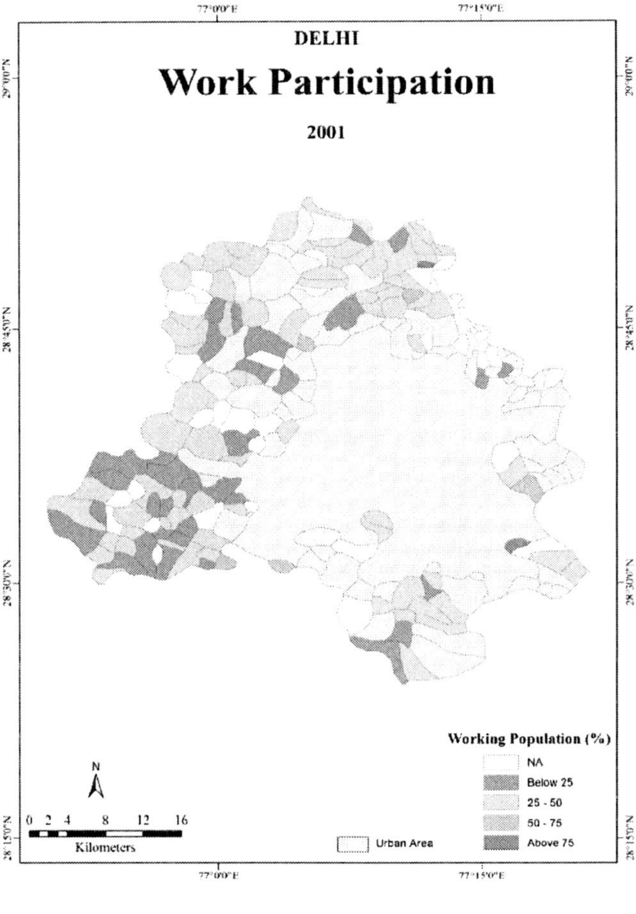

Figure 2.6: Working population in 2001

main worker, and those who had worked less than six months are termed as marginal worker. In the main workers male constituted more than female but in the case of marginal worker female are more. Among the all five blocks, Mehrauli block has highest per cent of total working population with 31.5 per cent followed by Alipur, Najafgarh and Kanjhawala and lowest is found in the villages of Shahdara block.

Table 2.10
Total Workers to Total Population (%)

Blocks	*Person*	*Male*	*Female*
Alipur	31.06	50.55	6.24
Najafgarh	28.97	47.76	6.05
Kanjhawala	28.40	46.72	6.05
Mehrauli	31.50	50.31	7.10
Shahadra	27.64	47.41	3.35

Source: Census of India.

In the case of male worker highest percent is recorded in the Alipur followed by Mehrauli, Najafgarh and lowest per cent of male workers is found in the block of Kanjhawala. As far as female worker is concerned Mehrauli's villages have highest per centage of female worker but rural area of Shahdara block has only 3.35 per cent female worker to the total population, while Alipur, Najafgarh and Kanjhawala blocks has almost equal per cent of female workers.

Table 2.14 reveals that per cent of female worker is more than male workers in all categories except cultivators but big gap of male and female worker is found in agriculture labourer category. The Table 2.15 based on the Central Statistical Organisation's data tells that in Rural Delhi 87 per cent female do not work according 1992-93 survey.

Table 2.11
% to total Main Worker

	Male	*Female*	*Total*
Cultivator	9.1	9.1	9.1
Agricultural Labourer	6.6	10.8	6.4
Marginal Worker	0.5	1.2	0.8
Household Industry	1.7	1.9	1.7

Source: Central Statistical Organisation

Table 2.12
Distribution of Rural Women by Employment Status 1992-93 (%)

Not working	86.9
Working in Farm	3.4
Working for some one else	6.0
Self employed	3.7

Source: Central Statistical Organisation

After the getting agriculture land and selling of land, significant occupational diversification has occurred. In the time when surplus land was distributed to landless persons economy of the villages was based upon particularly on land resource. "Jajmani" system was one of the caste related occupations of some castes like, barber, brahmin, potter, carpenter black smith, chamar etc. But with the passing of time this Jajmani system weakened. It may be pointed out that discontinuance of the "jajmani" system was not caused only by the change in the village economy but also because the younger generation of these castes have become conscious of social status and prestige. As a result a large number of families changed their traditional occupationon the ground that if they continue with these occupations, they will be considered as lower caste living on the mercy of land owners and rich families of the village. The villagers in the beginning increased their prestige through adoption and modifications in way of living and occupations to become distinguished among the ordinary villagers. More changes took place among the poor people who were basically agricultural labourers.

Figure 2.7: Medical facilities in Rural Delhi, 2001

Medical Facility

The medical facilities in the villages of Delhi are poor. The villages have to rely on the urban area for curing small diseases. The majority of villages do not have dispensary facility at all. Only 21 villages have medical dispensary.

Market Facility

Accessibility to market is an essential requirement for development of rural economy. Delhi with good connectivity of roads has good accessibility of markets. Only a few of villages are not having good connectivity to market (Figure 2.8).

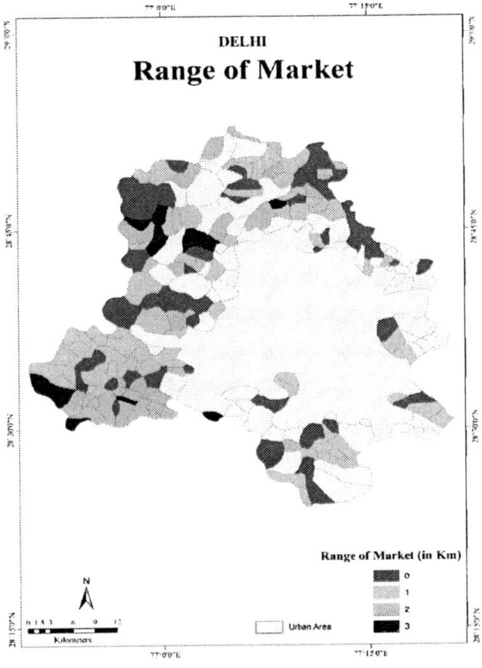

Figure 2.8: Marketaccessibility in Rural Delhi, 2001

References

Census of India. (1991), Primary Census Abstract, Part XII, A & B. Government of India, Delhi.

Census of India.(2001), Village Directory, Delhi. Government of India, Delhi.

Census of India.(2011), Primary Census Abstract. Government of India, Delhi.

Delhi Administration. (1976), Gazetteer of Delhi, Delhi.

Delhi Administration. (1987), Gazetteer of Rural Delhi, Delhi.

Delhi Administration. (1995), Bureau of Economic and Statistics, Delhi.

Dube, S. C. (1966), Rural Society, Abhinav Publication, New Delhi.

Gerald, M. Meier. (1976), Leading Issues in Economics, Devolvement, Oxford University. India Meteorological Department, New Delhi.

Rao, V.K.R.V. and Desai P.B. (1960), : A Study of Urbanization (1940-1957). Institute of Economic Growth, Delhi.

Srinivas, M.N. (1978), India's Village, Media Promoters and Publishers, Mumbai.

CHAPTER–3

RURAL DEVELOPMENT PROGRAMMES

Introduction

Rural Development is a wide concept encompassing all aspects of improvement in the quality of rural life. It implies both, economic betterment of the people and the effective social transformation. But in its limited interpretation, rural development has come to mean a direct attack on rural poverty through special employment programmes, land reforms and measures to provide safe drinking water supply and rural housing, sanitation etc. The need for rural development was emphasized even during the struggle for independence.

To achieve the aims of social justice and equality among citizens the country adopted planning as a policy of development and systematic efforts of rural development were started during 1952. The first step in this direction was the Community Development Programme (CDP). It adopted a systematic and integrated approach to rural development. The National Extension Service (NES) was established in 1953 with a view to reinforce the administrative network to tackle the problem of rural development. A new era in the realm of rural development was inaugurated when the Panchayati Raj Institutions were started in 1959, which became the basic institutional apparatus through which socio-economic transformation of rural area was to be achieved.

Programmes of development are always prepared by taking into consideration the needs of a particular population group, area and take notice of all relevant information to meet long felt needs as also their feasibility, given the necessary inputs like finance, technology, dissemination and over seeing. If the programmes do not make much heading, it is because of the fact that their implementation lacks one very basic element so necessary for the success of the programmes is the co-ordination among various wings of the implementation machinery and effective participation of people in programmes.

The early 1970 saw the formation of Marginal Farmers and Agricultural Labourers Development Agency (MFALD) with the main objective of taking care of the individual beneficiaries among the poor classes. This MFALD agency got new name of District Rural Development Agency (DRDA) in 1979-80, but in 1992, it was abolished in Delhi. Apart from the above programmes other implemented programmes includes Integrated Rural Development Programme (IRDP), National Rural Employment Programme (NREP), Rural Landless Employment Guarantee Programme (RLEGP), Assistance to Small and Marginal Farmers, Land Reforms, 20 Point Programme, Jawahar Rozgar Yojna (JRY), Training for Rural Youth for Self Employment (TRYSEM), Integrated Rural Energy Programme (IREP), Rural Water Suppty

Programme (RWSP), Rural Housing and Sanitation (RHS), Special Component Plan (SCP), and Integrated Development of Rural villages (IDRV) etc. These programmes were launched from time to time for upliftment of rural masses.

Small Farmers Development Agency

This agency was started in Fourth Five Year Plan (1969-74) with the specific objective of ameliorating the economic condition of small, marginal farmers and agricultural labourers also included who posses un-irrigated land upto 2 hectares and irrigated land upto 1 hectare. Agricultural Labourers includes those who earned 50 per cent or more of their income from hired work in agriculture. The functions of SFDA were (i) Identify the eligible small farmers in its area, (ii) Investigate and identify their problems (iii) Formulation programmes incorporating suitable measures to deal with the problems and (iv) Devise ways and means for implementing the programmes.

The category of weaker section was allowed subsidized loan for the following activities.

(A) Installation of the tube wells and pumping sets

(B) Purchase of milch cattle

(C) Establishment of poultry units

(D) Leveling of the land

(E) Soil Conservation

(F) Training of artisans

The subsidiary was given 25 per cent to small farmer and 33% per cent for marginal farmers and agricultural labourers. During 1979-80, this agency gave Rs. 10.8 Lakhs as subsidy to 1333 persons and Rs. 28.87 Lakhs for loans through nationalized banks.

Farmers Training and Education Scheme

This scheme was taken up in 1968 to impart training to farmers in mechanized cultivation and use of fertilizers, pesticide etc. Under this scheme, a training center was first set up at Alipur Block. During 1969-74 about 15,000 persons were got training under this programme; a new scheme related to women was started in 1975-76 to give the training to women workers to supervise the work of Mahila Mandals. The aim and objective of this schemes were:

1. Impart technical know-how about improved farms.
2. Prepare women for effective extension work.
3. Promote the leadership in women.
4. Create the awareness on family planning, improved nutrition, small saving etc. Rs. 9000/- for each 1979-80 and 1980-81 year was allocated in Budget for this scheme.

Rural Development Corporation

Simon Kuznet argued that agricultural development should receive top priority because cost effective production can be raised to make easily available in this sector than in any other sector. A rise in agricultural productivity precedes or accompanies economic development. Agriculture development is the core of rural development and without the desired progress and growth of this sector rural area cannot go on development path. Giving the emphasis on employment opportunities through agriculture and agro-based industries in rural area" DelhiAdministration has set up a Department of Development with following objectives.

A. Diversification of agriculture through encouragement of allied activities

B. Establishment of agro-based industries

C. Supply of agricultural inputs

D. Creating rural transport

E. Improvement of rural environment and housing facilities.

20-Point Programme

In July, 1975, soon after the Emergency was declared the Government introduced the 20-Point Programme which included a number of measures to improve the economic condition of the landless workers and other weaker section of the society in the village. These measures were:

(a) Speedy implementation of ceiling legislation and distribution of surplus land among landless labourers and small peasants.

(b) Provision of house sites for landless labourers and conferment of ownership rights of the houses.

(c) Liquidation of rural indebtedness and moratorium on recovery of debts from landless labourers, artisans and small peasants.

(d) Abolition of bonded labour.

That time landless labourers have been living a miserable existence. The 20 Point Programme was the first concrete step to ameliorate their economic condition and promote their welfare for rural development.That time late Prime

Minister Smt. Indira Gandhi ordered to all Gram Pradhan that they estimate the Surplus Gram Sabha land and distribute it among landless labourers and low caste people. Because that time most of the Gram Pradhan were belongs to upper caste in Rural Delhi they allotted this surplus land with biasness as in many villages land was also distributed to non-eligible families such as Brahmin Jat, Bania and Tyagi etc.

But on the other hand some Pradhan distributed with impartiality. People who had close approach to Pradhan got more agriculture land than others, Most of the agriculture labourers belonged to Harijan families. At the time of getting this land allotee had to face many difficulties. In the many villages of Delhi higher caste did not want to allot this land to Harijans. A good example of this event is "Kanjhawala Land Scandal". In this village Jat Community did not want that land should distribute to Harijan and low caste families so they gave the warning to kill all the allottee persons at that time law and order situation was very serious. Beneficiaries were restless 24 hours. For the help of Jat community of Kanjhawala, some people of this community came from Haryana and U.P. and other parts of country. For maintaining the law and order situations in this village, Government had to deploy CRPF. This matter has been continued for 2 years, ultimately Late Prime Minister of India Mr. Morarji Desai started his speech with this statement at 15 August, 1977 that land which was allotted to Harijan and low caste families, will not be taken. By this statement Jat Community got furious. Similarly other villages also faced another type of problems for getting agriculture land and ownership right.

During 1975 -76, 3,204 acres of agricultural land was distributed to 3,609 families out of this 2,162 were Harijans. Delhi land holding ceiling act, 1960 was amended in 1976 and under this act 1,916 bighas has been declared as surplus land and 5,851 bighas was declared as surplus land of category "C" i.e. unirrigated land. A number of cases of land distributions are under litigation as a result the land allocated to Harijan could not be utilized properly. In 1982-83 Delhi administration purchased 100 acres of land for allotting to 100 landless scheduled caste families. This land was free from all encumbrances and beneficiaries got the position to raise crops from the land allotted to them. Up to 1994, 1100 acres land was declared surplus and out of this 400 acres has been distributed to 900 beneficiaries. Now net area available for distribution is 160 acres (NIRD, 1996)

First time land was distributed in Delhi in 1975-76 and second time 1981-82. The beneficiaries of allotment of first time told that land which was allotted to them was infertile, barren undulating are not suitable for cultivation, so they had to work hard more and big invested agriculture inputs. This land took 3-5 years to be suitable for agricultural purpose. In Sabhapur village this land was given 10 km far from the village, beneficiaries told that although land was available but Gram Pradhan deliberately allotted it very far. After cultivation 5-10 years majority of beneficiaries sold it because of many reasons. But main reasons were encroachment of area by urbanization and re-settlement colonies and debt.

It was found by interview that this allotment of land broken the dependency on the Zamindar and they became independent for taking decision for socio-economic development. Before this land, Harijan and low caste people suffered torture of Zamindar. Delhi Development Authority acquired land of some villages for urban residential colonies and other purpose. The remuneration paid for the land acquired. Some beneficiaries used this compensation money for useful activities such as opening new business, building rent rooms and houses, but on the other hand some beneficiaries misused this money as they spent it in drinking, gambling and for luxurious life. Now their younger children are unemployed and have a low economic status.

In reality, this allotted land raised standard of living and developed socially them. Second time new 20-point programme .was announced on 14th January, 1982 by Smt. Indira Gandhi. It was a package of much needed social and economic measure to accelerate production and to reduce the hardship of the economic weaker section. It was agenda to promote social justice and economic growth. This was given the emphasis on schemes meant for the direct benefit and development of the poorer section of society. Under this new programme the families to be benefited in IRDP upto 1985 were 16,845 of which scheduled caste were 4,974 families.

Rural Development through Five Year Plans

After the independence our constitution, in its preamble, set forth the national objective of securing to the citizen of India justice andequality of status. To achieving these objectives the country adopted planning as a policy of development and systematic efforts of rural development were started since 1952. With the beginning of the First Five-Year Plan in 1952, a network of basic extension and developing services in rural areas was sought to be establishment at extending it to the whole of India. The experience indicated that in order to be sufficiently effective it needed strengthening. There was the concern that programme had more a significant impact on increasing farm productivity and rural employment that its benefits were accruing mostly to better endowed section of society. Therefore, programmes were designed for small, marginal, agricultural labourers and landless person. During Fourth Five Year Plan, Small Farmers Development Agency (SFDA) and Marginal, Farmers and Agricultural Labourers Development Agency (MFALDA) were initiated apart from this other schemes were also started as housing subsidies, improvement of Harijan Basties etc.Poverty alleviation oriented programmes, mainly IRDP, where undergovernment assistance is given as subsidy to identify families (having an annual income of Rs. 6400 or less) to enable them to eke out earning besides the facilities provided was launched in fifth plan wage employed programmes like National Rural Employment Programme (NREP) and Rural Landless Employment Guarantee Programme (RLEGP), TRYSEM, DWCRA were started in Sixth Five Year Plan. Under these programmes employment was given for unemployed person by engaging in labour work for the creation of community assets like village roads, school buildings, minor irrigation and social forestry etc. Upto Sixth Plan theschemes and programme of Rural Development were included under the section of Agricultural and Allied Services and in this VI th plan a total expenditure of Rs. 6,315 lakhs has been incurred. For the formulation of Seventh Five Year Plan for Delhi, Planning Commission proposed Rural Development as an independent sector. Planning Commission took the view that not sufficient numbers are reporting for work under NREP and like wise there appears to be no scope for RLEGP. Rs. 2 crore has been allocated in Seventh Plan to assist about 50,000 families living below the poverty line.

JYR, allotment of surplus land to landless labourers, development and construction of Panchayat Ghar etc. were implemented in Vllth Five Year Plan. In this plan period, 46 chaupals for scheduled caste 18, panchayat ghars, 418 bio gas plant were installed. Rs. 592 Lakhs has been spent on this sector which was 0.23 per cent of total amount of 7th Plan (Planning Commission, 1992). In Eight Five Year Plan emphasis was given an IREP and IDRV and in this plan 0.55 per cent of total amount of the plan was allocated to rural development sector. Present IXth plan (1997-2002) has proposed outlay Rs. 359 crores

Table 3.1
Plan wise Expenditure for Rural Development

(Rs. million)

7th five Year plan	*8th five year plan*	*9th five year plan (Proposed)*
59.2	247.5	3590.0

Source: Planning Commission

Rural development has always been one of the abiding concerns of the successive Five Year Plan. The essential issue is not whether the outlay for rural development during the Five Year Plan increased or decreased but it is regarding the proper allocation and optimum utilization of allotted fund. Late Prime Minister Mr. Rajiv Gandhi also expressed concern on several occasion that 80 per cent of the allotted funds under IRDP scheme went into wrong hands and 20 per cent actually reached the beneficiaries due to the inherent structure bottleneck in institutional, organisational and administrative set up.

Integrated Rural Development Programme (IRDP)

Initially, the Government had adopted different approach for rural development such as multi-level approach, Integrated Area Development approach and Special Area Planning and so on but evaluate study of above programmes shows that fruits of development have mostly gone to the better endowed areas and better off sections of the rural society. The provision of productive employment \o the rural poor on a sustainable basis has become an issue of priority. It was felt that this can be achieved only when there is integration of major section of the economy of rural area. Therefore, Integrated Rural Development Programme was started in 1978-79 to meet the requirement of poor masses of rural community.

Singh (1985) explained the concept of integration in rural development proposes five fold institutional integration viz. sectoral integration, spatialintegration, socio-institutional integration, technological-ecological integration and integration of objective functions.

Azad (1977) defined IRD as integrated development of the area and people through optimum development and utilization of local resources - physical, biological about necessary institutional, structural and attitudinal changes and by delivering a package to encompass not only the economic field i.e. agriculture and rural industries, but also the establishment of the required social infra-structure and service in the area of health, nutrition, education, drinking water and housing with the ultimate objective of improving quality of life of the rural poor. The IRDR aims at raising per capita income and standard of living of the rural folk, providing fuller employment, elimination of waste, achieving self sufficiency in agriculture, prevention of distress in rural areas and migration to urban areas, increasing farm productivity and generation of maximum employment.

This programme is being implemented through the District Rural Development Agency (DRDA). The basic objective of the scheme is to provide an opportunity to families living below the poverty line, to avail assistance in the form of loan, subsidy and training for generation of additional income under two sub programmes TRYSEM and DWCRA of IRDP making them cross the poverty line. The DRDA arranged loan through nationalised banks for the identified person who have chosen to take up various economic activities such as milch cattle, poultry, piggery and goat keeping, small shop etc. and provide subsidy 25 per cent to small farmers and 33 per cent to all categories of personincluding agricultural labourers. In the case of scheduled caste the subsidiary provided upto 50 per cent of the loan amount of Rupees fifty thousands and 31,493 families were identified for assistance by a survey in 1981 and out of this 8,790 were scheduled caste families:

Table 3.2
Identified families under IRDP

Blocks	*Small Farmers*	*Marginal Farmers*	*Agricultural laboures*	*Total*
Alipur	513	1268	6255	8028
Najafgarh	500	2143	6789	6553
Kanjhawala	510	2183	3354	6047
Mehrauli	196	583	6789	7568
Shahdara	75	627	2602	3314
Total	1794	6804	22902	31498

Source: DRDA

During the VI Five Year Plan of Delhi 16,845 families were benefited and in VIIth plan 1,500 families assisted of which 29 per cent were scheduled caste and 22.5 per cent were women beneficiaries.

Making a household survey of Sabhapur Village of Shahadra block few Jatav families were found those got loan for purchasing buffalo Rs. 3000/- was given to each identified family and out of this amount Rs. 1500/- was subsidiary. That time an average cost of a buffalo was Rs. 4500/- After purchasing the buffalo beneficiary startedto sale the milk arid earn money.

The IRDP has also suffered from certain deficiencies: no proper identification of beneficiaries, lack of infrastructural facilities, absence of technical guidance to beneficiaries, lack of co-ordination amongst the bank and block officials. Also, insurance claims of animals failed to be settled expeditiously. The time taken was approximately one year from the time the DRDA application form is filled up till the grounding of the scheme.

National Rural Employment Programme (NREP)

The national rural employment programme was launched in 1983 to overcome the problem of unemployment in Rural Delhi. It was implemented as a centrally sponsored programme on a 50: 50 financial sharing between the centre and state Governments. The main objectives of this programme were:

1. To generate additional gainful employment for the unemployed and under - employed person in rural areas.
2. To create durable community assets for strengthening the rural infra-structural facilities, leading to growth of rural economy and increase in income of rural poor.
3. To improve the nutritional status and standard of living of the rural masses.

The programme was implemented through the DRDA. The works were to be taken up for execution on the basis of a series of projectsand annual action plans were prepared by DRDA. During1984-85. 23,720 man-days of employment were created. 52,455 trees were planted and three tailoring centres were set up upto 1985. The programme emphasized on social forestry, construction of community assets like chaupals, libraries, community latrine and reading rooms, playground and recreational centres in the villages.

Table 3.3

Employment generated (million man days)

1984-85	*1986-87*	*1987-88*	*1988-89*
0.023	0.03	0.10	0.13

Source: NIRD

Rural Landless Employment Guarantee Programme (RLEGP)

This programme was launched in 1984 in rural Delhi. It was implemented by District Rural Development Agency. The objectives of this programme were similar to those of National Rural Employment Programme. But RLEGP was limited only to the landless, with guaranteed employment of 100 days in a year. The objectives of the programme were:

1. To create durable public utility assets for rural community.
2. To provide employment opportunities to rural landless person so that at least one member of every landless labourer family in assured employment up to 100 days.

In the year of 1984-85 11,000 man-days of employment were generated by construction of rural roads and filling up of ground depressions.

Table 3.4
Employment Generated Under RLEGP

(million man days)

1984-85	*1985-86*	*1986-87*
0.011	0.032	0.021

Source: NIRD

RLEGP has to provided employment during the slack agricultural season; the employment under the scheme came mainly during the busy season. This may be due to the tendency to utilise funds provided at the fag end of the financial year.

Training for Rural Youth for Self-Employment (TRYSEM)

Training occupies an important place in the efficient management of any development programme. Besides providing skills, training programmes bring about desired changes in the outlook and attitudes of trainee in tune with ever changing needs of the environment, the society and technology. Training, like education, is an investment in human resource management. The time, money and energy spent over this is bound to pay rich dividends like human tools for achieving social change and economic growth. (Rajendran, 1992) This scheme was launched as a centrally sponsored on 15th August, 1979. As the agricultural land wasdecreasing rapidly so rural youth need to be absorbed in avocation other than agriculture. Its thrust is on equipping rural youth in the age group of as over 18-35 years with necessary skills and technology to take up vocations of self-employment in different fields. The main objectives of this scheme were to provide technical entrepreneurial skills to rural youth from families below the poverty line, to enable to take up self-employment in various activities, service, industry and business sector. In 1990-91 DRDA has trained 105 rural youths.

Table 3.5

Total Number of Trained Youth under TRYSEM

Year	*Total*	*SC*	*Women*
1983-84	834	-	-
1984-85	887	-	-
1985-86	304	-	-
1986-87	624	173	438
1988-89	401	59	139
1990-91	105	-	-

Source: NIRD

Above Table depicts that since 1983 to 1991 3,155 youths were trained. In the year of 1986-87 seventy per cent were women and 28 per cent scheduled caste persons.

In Nangli Poona village 10 person got the training of poultry farming but after completing training loan was not sanctioned by theblock officials and bank so their training went in vain. This scheme was the part of IRDP. As per guidelines 10 per cent funds of the total allocation are earmarked for TRYSEM.

Development of Women and Children in Rural Area (DWCRA)

This was also sub-scheme of IRDP and was introduced in 1982- 83 as centrally sponsored schemes of the Department of Rural Development with UNICEF Co-operation.

In rural areas, women take up a wide variety of agricultural and non-agricultural activities. However, the conditions under which these women work have not changed much. It has rightly been indicated that special scheme would be needed to improve not only income level but also the working conditions of the rural women. The focus of the scheme has been the upheaval of the rural households with women as heads of the families and women member of rural families living below the poverty line. The programme also turned at improving the status of poor women in rural Delhi. For implementation of the programme Kanjhawala block has been selected first in rural Delhi.

The scheme included following seven points.

1. Immunization of Children.
2. Income generating activities of women.
3. Daily training to improve the antenatal and postnatal care of mother and children.

4. Disability prevention and re-habilitation using low cost aids and methods.
5. Pre-school education
6. Water and latrine facilities
7. Child to child activities

The first point i.e. immunization of children already has been implemented successfully and second scheme income generating activities for women is going on. Primary thrust is the formation of groups of 15-20 women from poor households at the village level for delivery of services like credit and skill training.

The scheme has been divided into three parts

A. Identification of the women and to encourage them to take up the activities for generating of income.
B. Training of women in different trades and
C. Establishment of units and to provide assistance in procuring raw material.

The cost of training to women group beard by the UNICEF. During the 1985-90 Rs. 23,81,000 was spent on this scheme and out of this Rs. 1,30,000 was given to Kanjhawala and remaining to Alipur and Mehrauli block.

Jawahar Rozgar Yojna (JRY)

Employment generation, particularly in rural areas, appears to be the most challenging task for planners and policy makers, providing wage employment to the rural poor has been an integral part of our rural development efforts. Various schemes of employment generation were taken up from time to time. Jawahar Rozgar Yojna was launched on April 1, 1989 by merging National Rural Employment Programme with

Rural Landless Employment Guarantee Programme. The Centre and the States/UTS in the ratio of 80:20 finance JRY. It has developed as the most important scheme for employment generation meant for those below the poverty line. Sixty per cent of the total allocation on a project under this scheme has been earmarked for payment of wages and remaining forty per cent for purchase of materials.

The primary objective of JRY was to generate additional gainful employment for the unemployed and under-employed person both male and female in the rural areas. Secondly objectives were creation of sustained employment by strengthening the rural economic infrastructure and over all improvement in quality of life of village people.

Thirty per cent of the JRY beneficiaries should be women and priority was given to scheduled caste families. Higher priorities to work which are required for infrastructure of poverty alleviation programmes like IRDP DWCRA and social forestry, soil and water conservation, minor irrigation, anganwadis etc. Wages under JRY were to be paid at the rate notified for the prescribed schedule of employment under the minimum wages act for the relevant works and may be paid partlyin cash and partly in food grain. Of the total funds allotted, five per cent should be on administrative expenses and 10 per cent on maintenance of assets. The remaining amount has to be distributed on the following lines: 35 per cent on the economically productive assets, 25 per cent on social forestry, 15 per cent on million well scheme and 25 per cent on other works like tube-well, road etc. In Kanjhawala 5 tube-well for irrigation were installed under this programme in 1989 and latrines were build for each scheduled caste family.

Table 3.6
Employment Generation Under JRY

		1989-93	*(million man days)*	
Total	*General*	*SC*	*Women*	*Landless*
0.872	0.319	0.168	0.087	0.298

Source: NIRD

During the household survey of Rewla Khanpur Village of Najafgarh block, it was found that 7 persons were identified under JRY but identified person told that they met many time to block officials for benefit but they were not get any type of benefit under this programme.

Development and Construction of Panchayat Ghar

In the rural villages of Delhi, there is a great demand for the construction of new panchayat ghar as well as development of the existing panchayat ghars to cater the needs of village people. In such panchayat ghars small library, reading rooms, adult centre, sewingcentre, dispensary, club etc. were also proposed to be established andthe halls of the panchayat ghar can be used for watching T.V. programmes. At the outset the scheme covered such villages where the panchayat were not in condition to construct new panchayat ghar or repair the existing ones due to the paucity of funds.

A model panchayat ghar comprise of big hall and atleast three rooms. The approximately cost of such panchayat ghar comes about Rs. 1.25 lakh. When the Eight Five Year Plans for Delhi was formulating it was suggested that construction of panchayat ghar in villages should be devetailed within the provision of Rural Landless Employment Guarantee

Programme. It has however not found practicable to take up construction work under the RLEGP as this programme envisaged provision for rural employment of labourer daily wages and did not cover the cost of material etc. Hence, the continuance of the scheme under Rural Development Programme was considered indispensable. Rs. 62.15 lakhs spent for 48 panchayat ghars in 1985-90 and an outlay of Rs. 375 lakhs wasproposed during the present Five Year Plan. There was another scheme"Community Development and Panchayat", under this scheme, it was proposed to construct new chaupal exclusively for the Harijans in such village where this facility of chaupal did not exist. This scheme will cover such villages in the beginning where there was no chaupal for Harijan people and Gaon panchayat is not in the position to construct such chaupal due to paucity of funds. During Eight Five Year Plan for such Rs. 74.04 lakh has been spent for 51 chaupals and Rs 350 lakh in proposed for IXth Five Year Plan.

Grant-in aid to Panchayats for taking up Development works

This scheme covered following works:

a. Maintaince and development of well and tanks.
b. Reclaimation of wasteland and bringing wasteland under cultivation.
c. Maintaince and protection of panchayat ghars
d. Construction of new bridges and chaupal.
e. Filling up of insanitary depression and leveling of lands.
f. Provision of store water drain and soaking pits.
g. Pavements of street in village.

Under this scheme Rs. 5000/- was given to the desirous panchayat and the panchayat was asked to contribute same amount either from their own funds or by raising loan through the nationalised banks. The work under this scheme was being executed by the Minor Irrigation Division with the assistance of the tecfonical staff. The another scheme was development of villages wells and hand pumps. Although Municipal Corporation of Delhi (MCD) has got a scheme for rural water supply where in it was proposed to provide water pipe lines to the various villages of Delhi. Yet implementation of this scheme for covering all the rural villages are likely to take considerable long time. However in case of emergency and failure of water supply, the hand pump remains the only source of water to fulfil the requirement of the drinking water of villagers. This scheme was incepted at the 1980-81 and now this is ongoing. Rs. 1035 lakh has been approved for the 1992-97.

Integrated Rural Energy Programme (IREP)

The pattern of energy consumption in rural Delhi has undergone or major change under the impact of urbanization, resulting in the reduction of rural areas by 14,800 hactres between 1970 and 1986. Cowdung has developed market potential and is, therefore not available freely to the landless. Collection of dungs in rural areas has by and large become a more time - consuming occupation and a health hazard due to burning of unconventional materials for the sake of energy. Those living in urban villages have better access to cooking gas, kerosene and electricity as source of energy. On the basis of relevant studies done as pilot surveys, etc. the annual requirement of biofuels, as energy source for the present level of Delhi's rural population, in placed at nearly 1.5 lakh tonnes of animals dung cake and 1.0 lakh tonnes for each of agricultural wastes and firewood (Solanki, 1988).

The number of people depending on energy for domestic cooking and heating will rise in future in rural areas of Delhi. Keeping in mind the requirement of villagers, Planning Commission had initiated Integrated Rural Energy Programme (IREP) in seven states of India and Delhi was one of them.

Alipur block was the first when this programme was started after seeing the success in this block, this was started in all five blocks of rural Delhi. The objective of IREP was to create awareness for use of non-conventional and energy saving devices in the rural area to save fossil fuel to make the environment pollution free. The kind of activities that have been undertaken under this programme are installation ofBio-Gas Plant, improved chullah and sale of solar cookers, installation of domestic solar water heating system and improved chullah etc.

Installation of Bio-Gas Plants

Bio-gas is being generated from dung. The villagers are usingmud chullah and cooking gas for cooking purposes. In addition to domestic bio-gas plants the Delhi Energy Development Authority (DEDA), set up and running the community type bio-gas plant at following energy complex sites.

1. Rewla Khanpur 2. Libaspur 3. Dera
4. Kanganheri 5. Bakoli 6. Palam
7. Mandoli 8. Burari 9. Gazipur
10. Nangloi

These are large size bio-gas plants for supplying cooking gas on cheap rate to rural poor households. Community bio-gas plants were installed on Gram Sabha land near by dairy colonies, these are commercialized by DEDA since 1995. The central Government is giving subsidy at the rate of Rs. 2 lakh per plant. Target of 25-community bio- gas installation has been proposed by 2002.

Wind Mill

For the promote and encourage use of water pumping wind will, the Department of Non-Conventional Energy Source had launched a national wide demonstration programme and implemented by DEDA in 1983-84. The project of wind mill has also been taken up with view tosave fuel and electricity particularly in the rural areas. The wind mill use mainly for minor irrigation and drinking water purposes. The main thing of providing subsidy is to promote and generate awareness of non-conventional energy devices among the rural masses thus to save the energy.

Improved Chullah Programme

Improved chullah programme includes construction of a smokeless high efficiently improved chullah in every house in the village. This programme was taken up in 1984-85 by DEDA, with a view to reducing deforestation and meeting the cooking energy crisis. Because the chullah will continue to be the basic cooking appliance for many more years in rural areas. Therefore, important method is the use of improved wood burning appliances. During Seventh Five Year Plan total 81,558 chullah were installed and these are giving satisfactory performance and saving big amount of money. The improved chullah programme envisages implementation of fixed as v\fell as potable models of chullha. The improved smokeless chullah can save 700 kilogram of fuel wood per household per year. It is better from health and environment point of view. In the IXth Five Year Plan of Delhi a target of 50,000 has been fixed.(Deptt. of Planning, 1997)

Solar Cooker Scheme

This scheme was undertaken by DEDA since 1983-84. Two type of subsidy was bring provided on the sale of solar cooker. The subsidy of central Government and Delhi administration comes to more than 50per cent of the cost of solar cooker. Since 1983-84 about 5,000 solar cooker have been sold in the rural area of Delhi.

Pressure Cooker

Under the I REP pressure cooker is also the device, which are helpful for saving the energy. Pressure cooker has been proposed to energy needs of the rural families and thus fulfills the major objective of the scheme. Upto next four years a target of 25,000 pressure cookers of 5 litres is proposed.

These will be provided to the poor folk in the villages through the identification of the beneficiary from Block Development Office.

Domestic Solar Water Heating System

This item is not popular in the rural areas upto the desired extent as it require tap water on the roof of house, which is not available in mostly houses in the rural villages of Delhi.

Solar Home Lighting PV System (SHLPVS)

SHLPVS is a device which provides solar electricity for operation lights and fan, T.V., for specific hours of operation per day 1 to 2 hours. This system is very useful for domestic use, farmhouses, community centre, schools and where conventional supply is unreliable or not available. 500 of such system is target for rural Delhi, by 2002. Mahatma Gandhi Institute of Integrated Rural Energy Planning and Development.

Keeping the need in mind for planned energy supply for overall development of rural sector, the Government of India initiated the IREP aiming at developing capabilities in the states/Uts. For this purpose Mahatma Gandhi Institute of I.R.E. Planning and Development was set up at Bakoli Village in Alipur block of Delhi and started functioning in March 1990.Objectives of Institute were:

1. To promote the ideas of Mahatma Gandhi for a holistic and human approach to rural development and in that context to promote the integrated approach for sustainable energy planning and programmes for rural development.
2. The provide training and research and development facilities for the planning and implementation for the I.R.E.P.
3. To impart training in the planning and implementation of IREP totrainees as well as to administration experts, specialists, field andoperational personnel at various level including national, state, district, block and village.

4. To provide establish data base in rural energy consumption pattern demand, supply and technology in different micro regions of the country and utilise this data as inputs in rural energy planning process.
5. To establish and develop facilities and methods suitable for dissemination in the rural areas.
6. To design and implement various types of studies in hardware and software as well as various social, economic, agricultural and voluntary establishment related to rural energy planning.
7. To design and develop educational programmes in the areas of rural energy, rural development and rural planning and management. For this purpose co-ordinating with suitable universities. (Plannning Commission, 1997)

Minor Irrigation

In the area of study, irrigation mainly depends upon ground water and partly on surface water is provided through shallow cavity, tube wells and whereas surface irrigation is by way of utilising treated effluent water from existing sewage treatment plant, water for irrigation purposes also gets from western Yamuna canal, but this is under the control of the Haryana Government. By the western Yamuna canal 3600 hectares of land is being irrigated, 803 hectares by utilising effluent water of existing sewage treatment plants and 33,450 hectare from ground water including 750 hectares from state tube wells and about 25,700 hectare from private tube wells. In Delhi, state tube wells were 190 and private tube wells were 14,000. Average area per tube well was 4-5 hectares.

Table 3.7
Amount allocated to irrigation (Rs. million)

		8th Year Plan	*9th Year Plan (Proposed)*
1.	Ground Water	3.49	23.200
2.	Surface Water	60.58	72.80
3.	Other Scheme	2.36	4.00
		66.44	100.00

Source: Planning Commission Ground Water Scheme

1. Providing Additional Deep Bare to Existing State Tube-Wells: This scheme provides additional deep bore to existing state tube well in Kanjhawala block of Delhi. The sallow cavity tube wells installed in this block are not yielding water due to the receding water table. Most of the shallow cavity tube wells have become in - operational. In order to continue providing irrigation facilities to the small and marginal farmers, the present scheme is being executed.

2. Deeping and development of ponds in village Mugeshpur and Auchandi: The water level is going down considerably in Delhi. In order to recharge the ground water resource, it is proposed to utilise theexisting depression and ponds in rural Delhi, to meet the requirement of local people for daily needs and would help in recouping the ground water level so an outlay of Rs. 10 lakh has been proposed to this scheme in 9th Five Year Plan.

3. Utilising existing storm water in Najafgarh drain for irrigation purposes: The Najafgarh drain is the main source of the pollution of river Yamuna in Delhi. In order to boost the irrigation potential of agricultural land in Najafgarh block, it was propose to utilise polluted water of Najafgarh drain. By this scheme 1000 hectares of agriculture land in Najafgarh block shall be benefited under the grow more food programme of Government of India.

4. Baprola lift Irrigation Scheme: As the Najafgarh drain passes through the thickly inhabited area of Delhi and it carriers lot of sewage artd polluted water, which flow, into river Yamuna. To control and reduce the pollution of river Yamuna has been a matter of concern of Delhi Government. Diversion of effluent water for irrigation purposes has been very helpful to curb the pollution of Yamuna. As such a lift irrigation scheme is proposed to irrigate about 24,000 acres of agriculture land of Najafgarh block, particularly Dichun Kalan, Baprola etc. by utilising storm water of Najafgarh block. The effluent water is manure rich and is instrumental in increasing the yield of crops and results in saving fertilizers.

5. Construction of soaking bunds/ tanks in rural area for ground water recharge: Due to development of large scale boring of tube -well in the rural Delhi during the last decade, the water level in the wells has gone down considerably, so in order to recharge the ground water resources, it is proposed to utilise the existing depression drains and tanks in rural areas for the storage of water. The work of construction of tank is proposed to be taken up in Nagafgarh and Kanjhawala blocks where the water table has gone down remarkably. For this scheme Rs. 20 lakh has been approved in the IXth Five Year Plan.

Integrated Development of Rural Villages (IDRV)

Delhi Development Authority (DDA), Municipal Corporation of Delhi (MCD), Delhi Vidut Board (DVB), Water Supply and Sewage.Disposal Undertaking, Flood Department, Health Services and EducationDepartment and other departments and agencies of Delhi Administrationhave been playing an important role of the development of rural areas of Delhi. The contribution made by the above agencies for the development of different sectors has not found upto desire extent. Keeping in view the ever-increasing population of the rural Delhi, the problems of these villages are required to be tackled in an effective way for better condition of rural Delhi. Taking into account the various aspects, the Delhi Administration has constituted a small working group in September 1984 for the preparation of Mini Master Plan for integrated development of rural villages under the chairmanship of Development Commissionerof Delhi. The infrastructure facilities like water supply, electricity, road, sewage, transport etc. are inadequate as compare to the present requirement of villages. No doubt, all the villages in rural areas in Delhi are connected by roads but the condition of roads in most of the villages has been very shabby due to lack of proper attention paid by the concerned department. Development of rural villages is not only involves the development department of Delhi Government but also many other agencies and institutes. The role of development department is to undertake such works, which have not been assigned to any other agency so that there is no duplication of activities. The objectives of IDRV were:

1. To protect Gaon Sabha land by providing fancing and new based amenities.
2. To develop community facilities
3. To develop industrial households industries in the rural areas so as to create more employment opportunities for the agricultural labourers and farmers.
4. To develop infrastructure facilities.
5. To develop commercial centres (Development Deptt. 1998)

This scheme was specially designed to improve the socio-economic status of the villagers of Delhi.

Mini Master Plan for Development of Rural Delhi: The mini master plan for planned and integrated development of rural areas of Delhi involving mainly construction of physical, social, economic and ecological infra-structure was conceived in mid-eighties. Later in 1992 a draft outline plan was prepared by Delhi Development Authority. The strategy involved in the plan has been to develop the entire rural areas as a "special area" based upon the concept of residential-cum-farm house. This shall ensure retention of both green character and ecological balance as well as development of area in a planned manner, so that haphazard growth can be checked and encroachment can be reduced to minimum. For the physical planning of the area, 195 villages have been divided into three tier. 15 villagesto be developed as growth centres 33 to be developed as growth points and remaining 147 as basic villages. This classification of villages was based on present population, growth of population, physical infra-structure, available social infrastructure, and potentiality for development and transport and communication components.

1. Growth Centre: Each growth centre will serve an area between 40-50 square kilometers, coming a population of 40,000 to 50,000 the type of activities to be called in the growth centre would mainly be of non-agricultural. Large areas will be developed for different types of purposes. Each centre will have a big shopping complex, a housing complex building of public and social utilities, small industrial estates and other types of facilities in the field of education, vocational recreational, banks, medical, health, sports centre, auditorium, restaurant, public conveniences, solar energy corner, mini forests, places for religious gathering, mandi, post office with telegraph facility, police statibn, cinema, storage for fertiliser, pesticides, veterinary hospital, bus terminal etc. All these centres willhave the facilities to serve population in the catchment area, as wellas neighboring area.

2. Growth Points: Each growth point will serve an area of 20-25 sq. km. covering a population of 15,000-20,0000. The growth point will have the facilities shopping centre of medium scale, primary, middle and senior secondary school, library, post office, telegraph, primary health centre, sportcomplex, multi-purpose community centre, public park and gathering and religious places.

3. Basic Villages: Each basic village will aim to serve existing abadi area where each basic village will have multi-purpose community centre with adjoining 8 to 10 shops, public park, primary school, sport stadium, public convenience, space for religious - cultural gathering, latrines, electricity and sub-post office etc. The mini-master plan is a long-term programme. The various project and scheme undertaken in the plan and going to extend up to the end of the Xth Five Year Plan. The master plan for IDRV was included for the first time in 1994-95. To begin with at micro level the task of construction of multi-purpose community centre in each of the rural villages was taken. The administrative and financial approval of construction of about 75 centres was issued to the PWD, MCD and DSIDC. In 1995-96, the preliminary work of development of three-growth centres at Kanjhawala, Bapraula and Chhawali kanganheri was initiated with the proposal to acquire land. In all a sum of Rs. 33.53 crores was utilized in the 1995-96 in construction of multi-purpose community centre and on release of money for land for growth centre. Annually Rs. 50 crores is given to this scheme.

1. To complete the spill cover works of multi-purpose community centre taken in hands in 1994-97.
2. To initiate construction of 25 multi-purpose centres in villages and the carry out development of 3 growth centres at Kanjhawala, Baprola and Chhawali, Kanganheri for which land has been acquired.
3. To initiate works for development of additional six growth centres and fifteen growth points.
4. To carry out works of laying trunk services viz. road, water supply, electricity and sewage disposal in the growth centre and growth point.
5. Re-development of village abadi of about 72-80 villages.

6. Carry out assessment, evaluation and monitoring.
7. Construction of individual toilet in premises of private households.

Special Component Plan For Scheduled Caste: The main thrust under "special component plan" (SCP) for scheduled caste was laid on providing economic assistance and improvemental facilities to scheduled caste families because these poor people were not in a position to earn their livelihood on permanent basis. Under this programme schemes are for shops, stalls, three wheeler scooters, loan for self-employment or enhance the business.

Delhi scheduled caste financial and development corporation, (DSCFDC), which was registered in 1983, approved loan to 2,902 scheduled caste families for taking up various vocational activities in 1983 -85. Out of the total loan 75 per cent was advanced by the State Bank of India and 25 per cent was provided by this corporation. Rs. 1.49 crores was released as special central assistance to special component plan for scheduled caste of rural Delhi in 1992-93 and Rs. 1.85 crores for 1993.94

Table 3.8
SC:Beneficiaries under Different Schemes

	No. of beneficiaries covered during 1980-85	
1.	Vocational and technical scholarship to S/C	3,000
2.	Free supply of book and stationary	1,56,925
3.	Subsidy for small scale and cottage industries	13,008
4.	Money for purchasing three wheeler scooter	700

Source: Planning Commission

For the poor scheduled caste students books and stationary was provided free of cost, during sixth plan 1,56,925 students were benefited. Apart from this, school uniform and scholarship is also given by the Delhi Administration. But this benefit is given after confirmation and fulfilling the prescribed provision by administration. For employment or enhancement of existing business corporation sanctioned the loan through S.B.I, with fix percentage of subsidy.

Assistance to SC Candidates for Poultry Training

The objective of these schemes was to impart training in modern poultry farming to scheduled caste persons. This was started under 20 - points programme in 1978-79. Time period of training was 15 days and during the training Rs. 375/- was given as stripened. During the household survey some trained persons were met in Nangli Poona village of Alipur block and they reported that they got training with stripened by block officials but after completing the training no loan was sanctioned for poultry farming ahd they were not in position to start this farming by own resources.

Balika Mandal

Balika Mandal was formed for the girl child of age group 15 - 18 years. The concentration is essential for social and mental development of girls to motivate them. The aims and objectives of this mandal are to make the adolescent girl, understand and learn the significance of personal hygienic, home nursing, first aid, health and nutrition, education and child care etc. The period of an adolescent girl's active enrolmentin the Balika Mandal vary one adolescent to another depending upon her previous educational background and her power to graps her possession of a home based skills and other activities.

The present existing Aganwadi Centre is to be used for the activities of the Balika Mandal. If there is lack of space in aganmadi then with the assistance of DWCRA and JRY another separate accommodation would be made. This scheme was started from 1st November 1991, in Kanjhawala block, and now it is running in Kanjhawala, Mehrauli and Alipur blocks.

Mid-day Meal Programme

Under this programme a nutrition meal is given to the children of nursery and primary school with following objectives.

1. To supplement the nutritional deficiency of the children.
2. To prevent children from purchasing unhygienic food them from hawker during recess time. \
3. To ensure reduction in the no. of absentees in the classes and encouraging for regular attendance.
4. This scheme was a part of Minimum Need Programme (MNP). The rate of the mid - day meal is Rs. 2 per child per day for 200 days in a year.

Rural Water Supply Programme

A national water supply and sanitation programme was introducedin 1954. The Government of India ordered to states to identify problem villages so that efforts could be directed towards tackling clearly identified problem villages.

Taking into account the magnitude of the problem and in order to accelerate the pace of coverage of problem villages, Government introduced the Accelerated Rural Water Supply Programme (ARWSP), in 1972-73 to assist the Delhi with 100 per cent grant-in-aid to implement the scheme in such problem villages. But with the introduction of Minimum Need Programme during the Fifth Five Year Plan, it was withdrawn. The programme of ARWS was however re-introduced in 1977-78 when the progress of safe water supply was not found to be as per expectation.

The national drinking water mission was launched in 1986. The mission was renamed Rajiv Gandhi National Drinking Water Mission (RNDWM). The following norms were being adopted for providing safe drinking water to rural population.

A. 40 litres of safe drinking water pe* capita per day for human being.

B. 30 litres of safe drinking water per capita per day additionally for cattle.

C. One hand pump for every 250 persons.

D. The water source should exist within area of 1.6 kilometer.

E. Water is defined as safe if it is free from biological contamination (Guina warm, cholera, typhoid etc) and chemical contamination (excess fluoride iron, nitrates etc.)

To this programme Rs. 6 crores has been provided during 1985-90.

In 1981, seven per cent of rural population was not availing the safe drinking water but this percentage reduced in 1991 as the 96 per cent population of rural Delhi was getting safe drinking water and 86.34 per cent availers were scheduled caste. But in reality the scarcity of water can be seen in Najafgarh block, particularly in summer season. For getting drinking water some time quarrel take place among villages. In summer season of 1998 many rural villages of Delhi faced the severe problem of scarcity of safe drinking water.

If water is life then sanitation fe a way of life. Both these are crucial for improving the quality of life and health. Rural sanitation covers disposal of waste water, human extra, garbage. Rural sanitation programme was launched in 1986 under NREP, RLEGP and Indira Awas Yojna. In 1988-89 Rs. 33 lakhs has been given for rural sanitation. According national institute of rural development, in rural Delhi there were 8 primary health centres, 42 sub. centres and 88 rural dispensaries in 1993.Industrialisation in Rural Delhi:

The strategy of rural industrialisation in India includes industrialisation of less developed area with the objective of correcting regional imbalance. This has been attempted through small-scale industries, cottage and village industries and attracting fresh investment in industrial ventures. Further, to promote the village and small industries, which were the major rural industries, a large number of developmental organisation, boards have been created to perform specific functions for the development of there individual segments (Chauhan, 1988).

The significance of rural industrialisation as a means for removing rural poverty and unemployment has been recognized as a major goal for rural development. Numerous studies have revealed that small-scale industries have great potentials for absorption of surplus labour out side the agriculture. Thus there is a need to promote rural industries.

The industries which were originally set up in rural area of Delhi with a view to rural development now Ijiave come to be a part of urban area for example Badli Industrial Area, Naraina, Mayapuri, Wazirabad and Nangloi etc. The industrial development in the Delhi has a rural bias since beginning so far the industrial were set up away from the city. During the second Five Year Plan period, Okhla Industrial Estate was established in a rural setting and in third plan period Badli Industrial Estate was set up to give impetus industrialisation. Shahdara and Najafgarh Road Industrial Area have served a similar purpose (Delhi Administration, 1986).

Emergence of Delhi as nerve centre of small scale industries has lead to the development of peripheral adjoining rural area i.e. Alipur, Najafgarh, Kanjhawala, Mehrauli and Okhla. Delhi had 8,160 units in 1960 but in 1986 it increased upto 62,000. In 1987-88 total number of handlooms were 1,761. The industrial policy (1982) for the Delhi brings out clearly the need for developing industrial activities in selected desirable directions. This policy lays special emphasis on promotion of industries particularly traditional industries, i.e., handicrafts, handlooms, Khadi and village industries and household industries. As per municipal bye-laws of Delhi, industrial units can be set up in Lai Dora of Rural Area only and not in extended Lai Dora and green belt.

Rapid urbanisation in rural area overtaken rural development. Urbanisation of rural area of Delhi has created socio-economic imbalance and conflicts among the rural people. Supreme Court of India has ordered to all haphazard and pollution spreading units to shift from thickly population area to another plac^e, so some of them are shifting in rural area and it will absorbs unskilled rural people to some extent, but it will pollute the rural environment.

Refferences

Azad, R.N. (1977), Integrated Rural Development in Dynamics of Development, Concept Publishing Company, New Delhi, Vol-2, pp 419-436.

Chauhan, D.S. (1988) Rural Industrialisation through small scale industries, cottage and village industries in Delhi in Science, Technology and Rural Development ed. by Lamba, P.S. and Solanki, S.S., Anmol Publication House, Mumbai.

Delhi Administration (1986), Gazetteer of Rural Delhi, Delhi

Department of Planning.(1997), Ninth Five Year Plan of Delhi, Govt, of Delhi, Delhi.

Development Department, (1998), Sardar Patel Gramoday Pariyojna, Govt, of Delhi, Delhi.

Datt, R, and Sundharam, KPM (1993), Indian Economy, S. Chand & Company Ltd. Delhi.

National Institute of Rural Development (1996), Rural Development Statistics, NIRD, Hyderabad.

Planning Commission (1992), Eighth Five Year Plan of Delhi, New Delhi.

Rajendran, R. (1992), Training in KVI, Khadigramdyog, KVI Commission, Mumbai.

Solanki, M.S. (1988), Energy and Rural Delhi in Lamba P.S. and Solanki, S.S. (eds.) op.cit.

Singh, R.B. (1985), Concept of Integration in Rural Development in India - Problems, Strategies, and Approaches Ed. by Singh K.N. and Singh D.N., National Geographical Society of India, Varansi, p.113.

Chapter—4

IMPACT OF DEVELOPMENT PROGRAMMES

Introduction

Rural development, being multi-disciplinary in nature and multi- sector in operation, is designed to fulfill multiple objective, viz more production, more employment, more equitable distribution of income, more infrastructure facilities, wider participation in the development process, increased access to modern inputs and services and greater self reliance and environmental awareness. It is viewed as an integrated process of planning and executing socio-economic and spatio-institutional changes in rural habitat consisting of people along with their cultural environment, spatial structures with their hierarchy, linkage and economicprocess with their faster inputs and product outputs.

The dimension of rural development, which are matter of all India and Third World concern command immediate consideration from planners and policy makers, professionals and technocrats. This sense of urgency steam from the growing conviction that the gains of development must reach the large majority of the population living in rural areas in more equitable, expeditious and systematic fashion. However the basic policies, processes and constraints involved in translating these concerns synthesized into policy against an unified development perspective and disaggregated afresh into modules and levels of implementation within a dynamic development frameare not sufficiently well understood (Rao, 1978).

Transformation in general denotes the subsitution or succession of one thing in place of another. Changes in rural context not only refers to the psychological attributes of human personality - attitudes, values, norms etc. The specific impact of change is the function of its magnitude and types of changes and the person's capability to tolerate it. The success of any development programmes depends as much on the response of those persons to whom it is intended as it depends on the organizational efforts to reach them. Numerous measures have been taken by the Government for the development of rural area, particularly weaker section of the village society. Administration has made efforts to provide suitable employment to the rural population through special schemes and programmes. Government is keen, naturally so, it find out the nature, degree and quality of rural response to development programmes. These have already been many attempts on the part of the Government body to assess the situation, through evaluatory studies of programmes on national level. A numbers of studies shows that benefits of the programmes have reached a certain stratum of society and those below it did not have capacity to take advantage of the benefits.

Only those persons in the village who have easy access to the block official are able to obtain assistant. The artisans, landless labourers, small and marginal farmers and poor masses for whomthe programmes were launched, received very little benefits. In comparison to other rural development programmes, allotment of surplus land to landless labourers, 20 Point Programme made significantly impact as by this programme socio-economic and political condition improved of beneficiaries of Delhi.

It is estimated that population of Delhi will reach 133 lakhs by 2001 and about 2 lakh persons migrate into Delhi every year and finally settle here. Employment is identified as the most important signal factor which attracts the people from other parts of country, particularly from Bihar, U.P., Haryana and Rajasthan. There is need to check this tendency of rapid migration. It is big challenge for administration to avail all the infrastructure facilities to all native. The problems of unauthorized colonies and J.J. clusters have increased tremendous pressure on basic services. Growth rate of rural population is increasing at very fast rate than of infrastructure facilities provided by the Government. Infrastructure includes all things provided by the Government, which promote directly or indirectly production activities like, transport, communication, water supply, education, health, irrigation, sanitation, etc. are considered important elements of infrastructure.

Rural villages of Delhi are not like the rural village of other parts of the country. The facilities which are available in urban area of other states can be seen in rural village of Delhi. They are also exposure of semi-urban life-style.

Table 4.1
Distribution of Villages of Delhi According to the Availability of Various Facilities

Facility	*No. of Village having facilities*
Education	178
Medical	89
Drinking water	195
Power Supply	199
Communication	199
Approach by Pucca Road	195

Source: Census of India

The Table 4.1 reveals that all inhabited village have power supply and communication but drinking water is available in 98 per cent village and 45 per cent village of Delhi have medical facilities. Although Government is trying to give all basic services in all villages.

Personal and Household Characteristics of Respondent

The personal and household characteristics of the respondent and the characteristics of their families have a direct bearing on socio-economic development.

Sex-Composition

In order to find out personal, household and socio-economic characteristics and perception of beneficiaries, a household survey of 200 benificiaries was conducted. 40 households of each block were selected. It was found that study area is male dominant as they constitute 58.2 per cent in total population.

Table 4.2
Sex Composition of Beneficiaries (Person in %)

Block	*Male*	*Female*
Alipur	59.3	40.6
Najafgarh	59.2	41.8
Kanjhawala	57.4	42.5
Mehraruli	56.4	43.5
Shahdara	58.4	41.5
Rural Delhi	58.2	41.8

Source: Personal Survey

In this survey total 1,144 persons were surveyed out of this 666 were male and 478 were female. Highest percentage of male person was recorded in Alipur and lowest in Mehrauli block. The gap between male and female is smallest in the area of Mehrauli and Kanjhawala block. Even today in rural area perference is given to male child birth than female. Each rural family want boy because they believe in Hindu mythology. However people also want minimum one - two girls because girl performed all the domestic function before marriage.

Majority of the respondents give equal right to boy and girl but few conservative families do not allow the girl for activity in every field and they provide limited sphere of area. Thinking about life - style of rural people is changing rapidly.

Caste Composition

Even today, caste play important role in rural society whole village society divided into caste system. There is clear-cut boundary between upper caste and low caste, like Brahim,

Jat, Rajput. Bania etc. are high caste and low caste are Chamar. Balmiki, Nai, Kasyap etc. In study area feeling of casteism is at very low level at present time but this level was higher in 20-30 years ago.

Table 4.3
Caste Composition of Beneficiaries Families

Block	*Lower Caste*	*Upper Caste*
Alipur	28	12
Najafgarh	31	9
Kanjhawala	34	6
Mehrauli	37	3
Shahdara	40	0
Rural Delhi	170	30

Source: Personal Survey

After primary survey it was found that out of 200 beneficiaries families, 170 belongs to lower caste and 30 belongs to higher caste.

There were found non-eligible higher caste families, they were also surveyed. Maximum upper caste beneficiaries were recorded in Alipur block followed by Najafgarh, but on the other hand Shahdara had none of them. When we co-relate caste to occupation income and education, we find there is positive co-relation, socio-economic condition of lower caste was poor. These families were mostly engaged in low income jobs.

Family Size of the Beneficiaries

Family being a backbone of any society provides necessary moral foundation. It is unit of social action. Large families provide economic security to its members who are very useful in case of unemployment and suffering. From beginning Indian society has been is representing the example of joint family but now a days it is breaking. For all socio-economic activities family is the basic unit. Thus family provides suitable physical, social and mental environment for a child to develop his skill - learn about customs, beliefs and sanitation. The overall development of any person depends upon the family to some extent. All the above mentioned functions of the family can get severe setback if the family is unstable and suffering from poverty, illiteracy, unemployment and conflict. On the basis of total numbers of person in family, all surveyed families were grouped into the three categories i.e. , small size family (below 3 members), medium size family (4-6 members) and large size family (above 6 members).

Table 4.4
Family Size of Beneficiaries in Rural Delhi

Categories	*No. of members*	*No. of families*	*% of total families*
Small size	1-3	36	18
Medium size	4-6	116	58
Large size	above 6	48	24
Total	200		100

Source: Personal Survey

Table 4.4 reveals that out of total surveyed beneficiaries household 18 per cent are small size and 24 per cent are large size but maximum households are of medium size, which are total 116 families. More than 50 per cent households of beneficiaries have 4 to 6 members in the whole study area. Earlier people believed that child is God's gift and they gave preference to have a big family. Poor persons considered children as an economic assets because after 10 years children started to help the family by earning something, and expenditure on bringing up was very small.

At present newly married couple want one or two children only, they are adopting the norm of small family. Rural people now want to give all necessary facility to development of children which is possible in the case of maximum two children. But on the other hand some very backward families have desire of large size family. It was observed from Table 4.4 that there is positive co-relation between size of family and size of house.

Family Size of Beneficiaries

Small size have 1-3 members Medium size have 4-6 members Large size have above 6 members

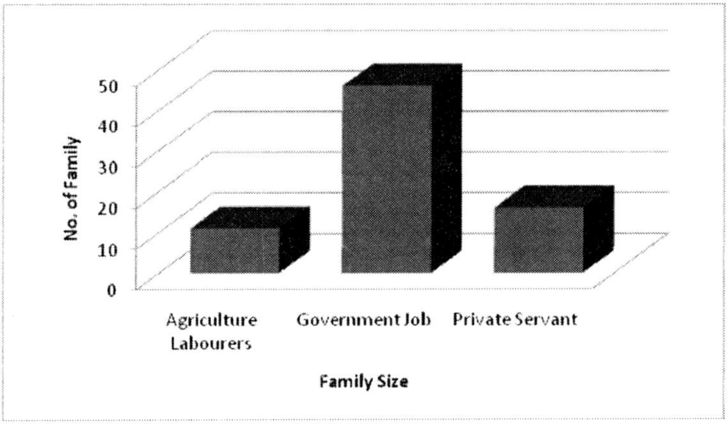

Figure 4.1: Size Wise Distribution of Families

Table 4.5
Distribution of Beneficiaries According Size of Family and House (percentage)

Category	*Small Size house*	*Medium Size house*	*Large Total Size house*
	(1-3)	(4-6)	(above 6)
Small size family	8.0	9.0	2
Medium size family	16.5	31.5	9
Large size family	4.0	10.5	6.5
Total	28.5	54.5	17

Source: Personal Survey

Medium size of family and medium size of houses have strong positive co-relation as they are 58 and 54.5 respectively. People with big families have constructed multi-storey houses in order to accommodate their large family.

Educational Status

Education holds the key to economic growth, social transformation and modernization and overall development after getting the education a person can get perfectness in his life and lead a better life. Spread of literacy and general education is the most powerful means of developing human resources. Close proximity of villages to the cosmopolitan centers has also benefited the rural sector. Delhi ranks third in literacy after Kerala and Chandigarh. The agrarian society,which was dominated by feudal elements prior to 1947, is being replaced by an industrial and urban society. The process of urbanization is usurping more and more agricultural land of rural Delhi. People have shifted their way of earning livelihood. Now agriculture is not the mainstay of the people living in rural areas of Delhi and there is major shift in economy and life style.

Out of the total surveyed population 26.5 per cent was found illiterate. Among illiterate maximum were old age persons. Maximum illiterate were identified in the villages of Shahdara and minimum in Kanjhawala block. Due to illiteracy they don't know about the development programmes. Literary rate of an area depends on a number of factors such as socio-economic condition of people, facility of school etc. In order to find out educational status of beneficiaries of study area five categories of educational level were made i.e. (I) education up to 5 class, (II) 6 to 8 class (III) 9 to 12 class (IV) B.A. to M.A. and (V) others. These categories are correspondence to less educated, moderately educated, highly educated, very highly educated and professionals (doctors, lawyer, teacher, manager and I.T.I, trained etc.) respectively.

Table 4.6
Educational Status of Beneficiaries (%)

Name Block	*Illiterate*	*less educated*	*moderately educated*	*highly educated*	*very highly*	*others educated*
Alipur	21.9	14.2	18.6	28.0	8.5	8.5
Najafgarh	21.4	15.3	20.0	28.9	0.8	13.1
Kanjhawala	19.6	9.5	11.9	44.4	10.0	4.3
Mehruali	31.6	16.0	20.0	25.2	2.6	3.9
Shahdara	37.6	21.6	14.2	19.4	1.7	5.1
Rural Delhi	26.5	15.4	17.2	28.9	4.7	7.0

Source: Personal Survey

It can be concluded from Table 4.6 that among the literate, maximum are highly educated persons followed by moderately educated and less educated. Among the all five blocks Kanjhawala has highest percentage of highly educated and Alipur and Najafgarh both have similar percentage of highly educated persons. Like previous category, very highly educated are maximum in Kanjhawala and Alipur has second rank with 8.5 per cent. Maximum literates are in Kanjhawala, the reason behind it is that Kanjhawala which has taken in household survey is not rural village; according to census of India it is a census town. Socio-economic development of Kanjhawala is higher than the other sample villages of study area. Rural masses of the sample villages wants to get education to a certain level, even poorest persons also wants to get basic education, after 12th class most of students drop out their education due to low economic conditions offamily and wants to get employment in various sector. A few per cent of students have continued their education by taking admission in I.I.T and college etc. Poor families sending their children in

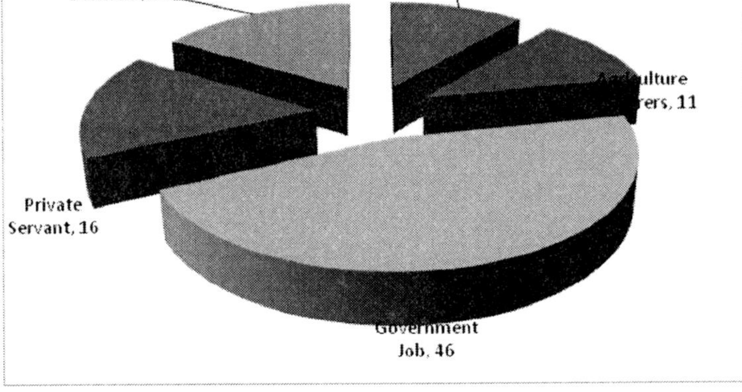

Figure 4.2: Educational Status of Beneficiaries

Government school of M.C.D. while some higher caste rich families sending their children in pubic and english medium school, therefore rich family is spending more on childern's education than poor household.

Largest percentages of school going children are getting education in government schools in Hindi medium. Now-a-days school teachers are not accountable and they do not teach with dedication and honesty. The results of Government school of rural area are not satisfactorily and percentage of passing student is decreasing. On the other hand children who are getting education in public school are more intelligent and showing better results. Students of rural area cannot competition to urban area students. Teaching of Governmentschool affects the socio-economic conditions of life because a child if he gets good education then he can compete any competitive or entrance examination and lead a better life.

Occupational Structure

Occupation refers to the type of work carried out by the beneficiary in order to earn his livelihood. It has direct bearing on socio-economic conditions of people. This structure of occupation has been divided into two parts.

(1) Pre-benefits of programme

(2) After benefits of programme.

Here meaning of pre benefits is condition of beneficiaries when agricultural land was allotted to them and after benefit of programme refers the situation of the mid year of 1998 when the survey was conducted. Total working population of surveyed households categorized into five categories namely agriculture labourers, Government servant, private job, business and other.

Table 4.7
Occupational Composition of Beneficiaries
[Pre benefits of Programme

Block	*Agri. Labour*	*Govt. Servant*	*Private job*	*Business*	*Other*
Alipur	61.5	10.2	7.6	5	17.9
Najafgarh	39.0	26.0	13.0	-	21.7
Kanjhawala	32.5	65.0	-	-	2.5
Mehrauli	45.0	25.0	3.0	12.5	10.0
Shahdara	65.0	15.0	-	7.5	12.5
Rural Delhi	48.2	28.2	12	4.8	13.0

Source: Personal Survey.

Table 4.7 indicates that before the allotment of surplus land Shahdara block's villages had highest percentage of agricultural labourers, followed by Alipur block, while lowest percentage was recorded in Kanjhawala. Considering rural Delhi as a whole, agricultural labourers, constitute largest segment of working population and second strength was of Government servant. That time mostly land owned people were "Zamidar" belongs to higher caste and landless, low caste family's work on their field for survival of life. Because at that time Government vacancies were more so masses got services of lower grade in various departments. Kanjhawala block had maximum number of Government servant. The category of other include inheritant job, daily wages jobs etc. In this category Najafgarh had largest percentage. Agricultural labourers reported that they were exploitedby landlords because of dependency. After the hard work of whole day they got very low wages which was not enough to meet their family's daily requirement. Low wages resulted in poverty and low standard of living. Few suffered person who are alive told that they devoted their whole life for Zamidar.

Present Occupational Structure

Occupation profile of present time of beneficiary families has got sharp changes and showing better result. Before the benefits of programme, rural masses of surveyed villages were engaged in primary activities and a few per cent were in tertiary activities but now more respondent are working in secondary and tertiary activities.

Table 4.8
Present Occupational Structure (%)

Block	*Agri. Labourers*	*Govt. Servant*	*Private Job*	*Business*	*Farming*
Alipur	8.4	38.6	15*	21.6	16
Najafgarh	11.7	44.7	12.9	10.5	20
Kanjhawala	3.7	67.5	15.0	3.7	10
Mehrauli	13.1	32.8	19.7	31.5	2.6
Shahdara	17	48.7	19.5	12	2.4
Rural Delhi	10.7	46	16.3	16	10.7

Source: Personal Survey

Present occupational structure reveals that out of total working population largest percentage of people are employed in Government services in different departments, institution and agencies while in pre benefit of programme about half of the total working population were agriculture labourers and second were Government servant. There is equal percentage in two couples. 1) Private job and Businessmen 2) Labourer and Farming. 2/3 of working population of Kanjhawala are employed in Government services. Among the all five blocks Mehrauli has biggest percentage of businessmen. There are some low educated and unskilled people who work manually in farm, factory and private firm. Table 4.7 and 4.8 show that rural masses have sifted from primary activity to secondary and tertiary activities. After selling the agricultural land beneficiaries started to set up new business such as shop, small scale industry, factory and other type of business. Less educated person are maximum in Shahdara and Mehruali block so there is also found maximum daily wage worker. Less educated people are minimum in Kanjhawala that is why this block has lowest percentage of labourers. Therefore there is co-relation between less educated persons and labourers.

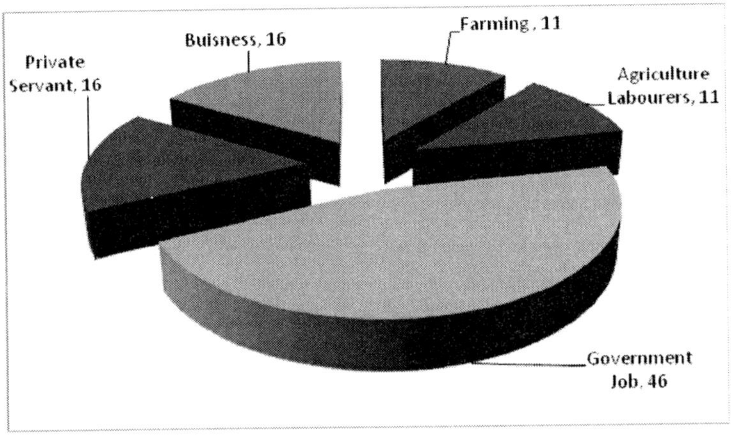

Figure 4.3: Occupational Structure of Beneficiaries

Most of the beneficiaries sold the allotted agricultural land due to various reasons. Delhi Development Authority constructed a network of re-settlement colonies on acquired land. After acquisition andselling the land farmers have no option except engagement in secondary and territory activities. But in some villages farming is going on. In present context, maximum farmers working in the agricultural land are found in the villages of Najafgarh and Alipur block as 80 per cent and 57.5 per cent respectively. But on the other hand in Shahdara and Mehrauli block have only 2.5 and 5 per cent beneficiaries cultivating their land because in these block land was acquired and purchased for rehabilitation colonies, community purposes and farm houses.

It can be concluded from above discussion that economy of rural Delhi has moved from primary to secondary and tertiary occupations. Mostly 80 per cent Government servant are sweeper lower/upper divisional clerk, and in low grade services. A few per cent are A and B grade officer. Rural youth reported that in spite of 42.5 per cent reservation in services for scheduled caste and other backward class, they are not getting any permanent job.

Income Status of the Households

Income is one of the most important means which raises the socio-economic status of the people and improve the standard of living. It helps people to meet their day to day requirement. Author has estimated the annual income of earning members from main source of income. To find out per capita income annually, gross income was divided by the total members of family, so here per capita income has been calculated for each surveyed household.

Per capita incomes of the families have been divided into four categories.

1. Low income group Less than Rs.6,000/-
2. Middle income group Rs. 6,001 - 15,000
3. High income group Rs. 15,001 - 30,000
4. Very high income group Above Rs 30,000

Table 4.9

Classification of Per Capita Income Group Annual (%)

Block	*Low income Group*	*Middle income Group*	*High income Group*	*Very high income Group*
Alipur	7.5	25	40	27.5
Najafgarh	5	27.5	60	7.5
Kanjhawala	0	37.5	37.5	25.0
Mehrauli	0	52.5	42.5	5.0
Shahdara	0	40.0	47.5	12.5
Rural Delhi	2.5	36.5	45.5	15.5

Source: Personal Survey.

Table 4.9 indicates that in sample villages of rural Delhi maximumfamilies belongs to high income group followed by middle incomegroup and very high income group so high income and middleincome group constitute more than 80 per cent of total household.

In Najafgarh 60 per cent of the beneficiaries belong to high income group or in other words they earn between Rs. 15,001 to 30,000 annual per capita. In the category of very high income Alipur has first rank and Kanjhawala, Shahdara has second, third rank respectively. In this group a few non-eligible household were also found. Except Mehrauli block

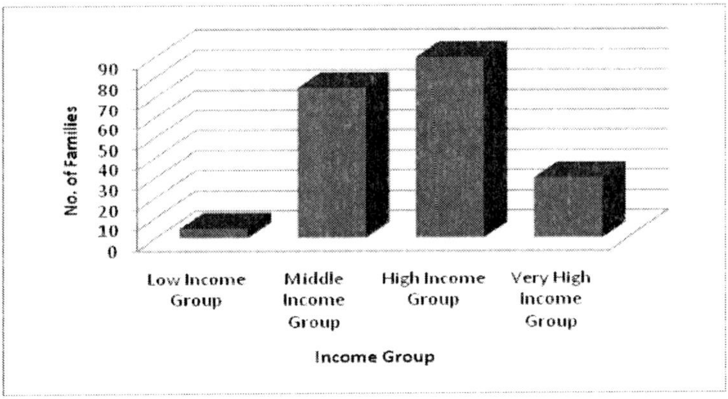

Figure 4.4: Per Capita Income Groups (Annual)

all block of rural Delhi has largest percentage of high income group.

Before the benefits of programme the percentage of familiesof low income group was high but after the benefit, middle and highincome groups constitute the largest percentage. Per capita incomeinfluence by the total number of members because if total members are more then per capita income will less. 20 point programme under which surplus land was distributed really benefited the people in social and economic aspects as it has broken the cycle of dependency on "Zamidar". Beneficiaries told that this land provide food grains for the need of family and earn money by selling surplus production and get fodder for animals for whole year. Apart from this others schemes and programmes helped in raising standard of living.

Debt and Savings

During the household survey, it was found that most of the families had to borrow money from outside to meet both then ends. This money was taken mostly from Zamidar. Borrower had to give interest. Earlier most of the families were poor so they were not in position to complete any big function without economic assistance.

Table 4.10
Debted Beneficiary Families (%age of families)

Block	*Pre-benefits*	*After benefits*
Alipur	45.0	27.5
Najafgarh	57.5	25.0
Kanjhawala	55.0	22.5
Mehrauli	72.5	10.0
Shahdara	77.5	20.0
Rural Delhi	61.5	21.0

Source: Personal Survey.

Table 4.10 shows that before benefits of programme 61.5 per cent of beneficiaries were under debt in rural Delhi and maximum were in Shahdara block's village and minimum in the villages of Alipur. At present context, percentage of debted families has gone down which is 21 per cent. Now Alipur has maximum debted households while in pre-benefits it has last rank. Mehrauli shows best result as it has 72.5 per cent debted household earlier but now it has only 10 per cent. One thing is clear that in all five blocks number of debt having families reduced. Present data itself representing that peoplegot really benefitted from 20 Point Programme. A few beneficiaries reported that in beginning, to prepare the agriculture land for cultivation more inputs had to apply so they had to borrow some amount of money and they became debted. Survey analyses that a big percentage of people sold their agriculture land due to debt. Untill the beneficiaries did not get benefit by programme, only 17 per cent families were able to save some money. Now 145 households out of 200 are saving money for future.

Table 4.11
Families Have Saving of Money (%)

Block	*Pre benefit*	*After benefit*
Alipur	25.0	70
Najafgarh	15.0	80
Kanjhawala	15.0	75
Mehrauli	12.5	65
Shahdara	17.5	72.5
Rural Delhi	17.0	72.5

Source: Personal Survey.

Before the benefits of programme village of Alipur had maximum saver of money followed by Shahdara, Najafgarh, Kanjhawala and Mehrauli block but now Najafgarh has first rank followed by Kanjhawala block. Some respondents told that about 25 years ago they could save some money but today prices is rising so it is not possible for them to save some money. Figure 4.6 shows that there is negative co-relation between debt and saving, if debt reduces then saving increases.

Loan

Loans are taken for increasing source of income and perform all the necessary functions. Some schemes were implemented from time to time by Government to raise the income of needy person, such as loan on subsidy, free

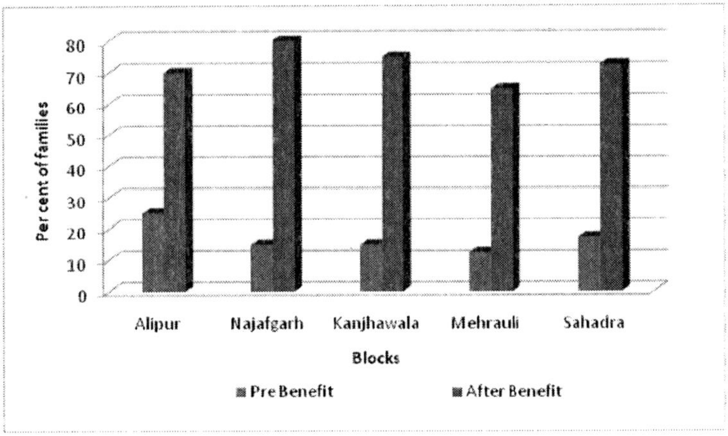

Figure 4.5: Saving by Respondent

Figure 4.6: Debt and Saving in Rural Delhi

interest loan etc. After completing the household survey of 200 families of rural Delhi, it was pointed out that 21.5 per cent families had got loan for various purposes. Granted loan was classified into three category as shown in Table 4.11. Maximum families had taken loan for buffalo followed by shop / vehicle and house construction. Najafgarh block had occupied first position in terms of granting the loan and last rank has Kanjhawala where only 4 families out of 40 has got the loan.

Table 4.12
Loan Taker Families (%)

Block	*Buffalo*	*House Construction*	*Shop / Vehicle*	*Not taken*
Alipur	5.0	0	15.0	80
Najafgarh	17.5	12.5	2.5	67.5
Kanjhawala	2.5	7.5	0.0	90.0
Mehrauli	5.0	0	10.0	85.0
Shahdara	17.5	2.5	10.0	70.10
Rural Delhi	9.5	4.5	7.5	78.5

Source: Personal Survey.

In Najafgarh and Shahdara block seven families in each were identified, as benefited by loan for buffalo and after getting loan they purchased buffalo and started to sell the milk and generate new source of income. For opening new shop and purchasing the public goods carrier maximum loan taken were found in the villages of Najafgarh followed by Alipur block.

As far as house construction loan is concerned five beneficiaries were recorded in Najafgarh and three were in Kanjhawala when we co-relate the loan to the saving then we found that after getting loan sixty five per cent beneficiaries started savings because this loan create new income source of income or enhance family's income. This loan was granted by any schedule bank after detailed inquiry. Better result was come from beneficiaries who had taken loan for shop or vehicle as ninty three per cent started savings of money while this figure for buffalo was fifty three per cent. Families whowere living in kutcha house the built pacca house after getting loan.

It can be concluded that impact of loan on economic condition was positive. This loan increased the income and capacity for savings. Getting loans by poor people was not easy task. If needy person does not have approach or link to the officials then it is not possible to avail this facility. Younger unemployed people criticised the Government policies that if any body wants to set up own business then on each and every step officer demand bribe and failing leads cancellation of application form if loan sanctioned then middle men start the demand of commission. Therefore, respondents reported that before taking loan some amount of money has to give as bribe.

Agricultural Land

The agricultural base in rural areas of Delhi has undergone many changes since independence time. Total cropped area has gone down as it was 1,13,482 hectares in 1960 and 76,239 hectares in 1991. During four decades many changes have been witnessed in the agricultural pattern of Delhi. Technological development in agriculture have brought in more intensive practices, larger areas have been brought under irrigation, cropping pattern has changes in favour of better yielding grain crops. Naturally these changes have resulted in prosperity and improvement in living standard for those who still owned agricultural lands (Lamba and Solanki, 1988).

Table 4.13
Situation of Alloted Land (%)

Block	*Cultivating*	*Sold*
Alipur	57.5	42.5
Najafgarh	80.0	20.0
Kanjhawala	40.0	60.0
Mehrauli	5.0	95.0
Shahdara	2.5	97.5
Rural Delhi	37.0	63.0

Source: Personal survey

It can be inferred from Table 4.13 that land which was given to 200 beneficiaries now thirty seven per cent are cultivating and remaining sold it or acquired by Government. Eighty per cent of the beneficiaries in Najafgarh block still peruse agriculture, followed by Alipur. In Shahdara and Mehrauli very low percentage of beneficiaries engage in agricultural activities. Particularly in south and eastern rural Delhi primary occupation has declined over the years. People now want to adopt jobs which are more lucrative and hence are engaged in secondary and tertiary activities.

At the time of allotment of land, more people were engaged in agriculture and almost all rural families had buffaloes for domestic need. Milk was considered very important thing in villages and fodder could get free from field.

Table 4.14
Number of Buffaloes

Block	*Pre benefits*	*After benefits*
Alipur	79	36
Najafgarh	78	50
Kanjhawala	60	15
Mehrauli	123	45
Shahdara	86	31
Rural Delhi	426	177

Source: Personal Survey

Before the getting of surplus agricultural land 200 households had 426 buffaloes but now this figure has gone down to 177. Earlier Mehrauli block's village had largest percentage of buffaloes followed by Shahadra, Alipur and Najafgarh but now Najafgarh occupies first rank as it has 28 per cent of fatal.

In Najafgarh and Alipur block percentage of buffalowes increased but absolute numbers decreased. The respondents of Kanjhawala, Nanglipoona and Gharoli reported that although they want to keep buffalo but space and fodder is not available for them. As the agricultural occupation is going on in Najafgarh and Alipur so they avail free and abundant fodder from field so they have buffalo according to their capacity. Decreasing the number of buffaloes show that economy is moving from primary to other activities. Eachrural household wants to keep minimum one or two buffaloes for domestic need. 84 per cent households have less than two, 12 per cent have 3-4 and 4 per cent have more than 4 buffaloes.

Table 4.15
Reasons of Agricultural Land being sold

Block	*Fear of Debt Acquitement*	*Own desire*	*Acquired*	*Other by Govt. reason*	*(% of families)*
Alipur	23.5	35.0	11.7	17.6	11.7
Najafgarh	0	62.5	25.0	0	12.5
Kanjahwala	16.6	50.0	33.0	0	0
Mehrauli	21.0	47.3	31.5	0	0
Shahdara	0	25.6	23.0	17.9	33.3
Rural Delhi	12.6	40.4	26	7.9	12.6

Source: Personal Survey.

Table 4.15 represents that forty per cent of beneficiaries sold their land due to debt followed by own desire (26%) and fear of acquirement (13%).

Reasons why rural masses had to leave agriculture occupation land are as follows:

1. In the villages of Mehrauli and Shahdara people faced great difficulties. Beneficiaries of these blocks told that agricultural land was allotted in sandy area of Yamuna and in hilly area. Sabhapur's beneficiaries got this land 10 K.M. far from residence surplus land was available, therefore due the farness and sandy soil people sold it at very low rate. Beneficiaries of Jonapur village reported that allotted land was very undulating and unfertile. The return output was less than input.

2. For making it fertile land in beginning they had to invested more inputs and for this they had to take debt from outside. Diseases, marriage's expenditure increased the debt so for paying the debt 40 per cent beneficiaries sold the agricultural land.

3. In some villages like Jonapur, Nangli Poona and Qamurrudin Nagar, Gram Pradhan and some other dealer spreaded the misinformation that land of these villages will be acquired by Government for community purpose so some beneficiaries farmer feared and they started to sell it at lower rate. If Gram Pradhan helps in purchasing land from farmers then he gets some commission from dealer, colonizer and owner of farm house. Now on this land re - settlement colonies, farm houses and factories etc. can be seen.
4. In Gharoli village land was acquired by DDA to build flat. Land of 3 beneficiaries were acquired for G.T. Road in Nangli Poona, land of other villages of Delhi also acquired for residential cum institutional purpose by DDA such as Rohini. DDA took this land at floor prices and sell it at sky high prices. Villagers were just ignored and no developmental schemes were taken up for them. At the time of acquiring land DDA promised the farmers that better compensation, alternative plot and one employment in each household of farmer will be given. But after long legal battle they got very low remuneration as 50 paise to Rs. 2 per sq. yard, the price of alternative plot was beyond the reach of farmer and it was allotted very far from beneficiary's home. As few farmers of Badli village get allotment of plot in Narela. No employment was given to them. For getting compensation every farmer had to go through complicated procedure from lower court to Supreme Court. This

compensation money utilized for various purpose by villagers.

5. 26 per cent sold it by personal desire including family's conflict - tension, need of money, not to be profitable.
6. Besides this there were also other strong reasons that scarcity of irrigation water, lack of personal mechanised equipment, increasing encroachment around the agricultural field etc.

Now agricultural land is diminishing at fast rate. Agricultural land is going to use for commercial and non-agricultural uses. Small farmers want to give up this profession owning to many reasons.

Table 4.16
Families Faced Problems in Getting Allotment of Agriculture land (% age of families)

Block	*Total no.of Families*	*Per cent of families*
Alipur	15	37.5
Najafgarh	12	30.6
Kanjhawala	23	57.5
Mehrauli	18	45
Shahdara	21	52.5
Rural Delhi	89	44.5

Source: Personal Survey.

To reduce poverty in lower caste masses surplus land of Gram Shaba was distributed among landless farmer. Before this allotment they worked on Zamidar's field. The sociological and socio-anthropological studies provide enough evidence to prove the fact that the extent of ownership of land is an important indicator of one's socio-economic status (Mohammad, 1988).

At the time of allotment mostly Gram Pradhan of Delhi werebelonging to higher caste some of them did not want to provide thisland to lower caste people. Through survey it was pointed out that44.5 per cent beneficiaries faced the problem for allotment. Morethan fifty per cent beneficiaries of Kanjhawala and Shahdara blockfaced it in rural Delhi. Respondents reported that for getting allotmentthey had to fight with higher caste families and conflict and tensionwas also took place between higher and lower caste. Some GramPradhan allotted this land with partiality because they also allotted thisland non-eligible person who had already more agriculture landbelongs to upper caste such as Jat, Pandit, Bania, Yadav etc.

In Badli village 1/2 killa of (2 bighas and 8 bisma) agricultural land was allotted to each lower caste eligible family while more than 1 killa to Yadav and Brahmin because Gram Pradhan was Yadav. In other villages of Alipur block, the land was also distributed to non- eligible households. On the other hand a few Pradhan distributed this according rule and regulation without any biasness. Being in spite of available surplus land in villages some Pradhan told to the official body that villages have no surplus land.

Socio-Economic Amenities

To find out socio-economic conditions a list of indicators was prepared for survey, such as radio, telephone, scooter, car, refrigerator, sofa, bath room, toilet, cooking gas, housing condition etc.

Table 4.17
Families having Different Amenties (% age of families)

Block	*Vehicle*	*Refrige-rator*	*Telephone*	*Double Bed*	*Sofa*
Alipur	25	47.5	30.0	50.0	45.0
Najafgarh	15	45.0	12.5	32.5	22.5
Kanjhawala	35	72.0	27.5	70.0	57.5
Mehrauli	32.5	65.5	27.5	67.5	55.0
Shahdara	37.5	40.0	20.0	37.5	32.5
Rural Delhi	29	54.5	23.5	51.5	42.5

Source: Personal Survey

Domestic amenities shows that more than fifty per cent beneficiaries have refrigerator and double bed, twenty nine per cent have vehicle and twenty three per cent have no personal telephone. While before the benefits of programme none of them had any amenity of mentioning above. Shahdara, Kanjhawala and Mehrauli's beneficiaries have more vehicle than Najafgarh and Alipur. In Qamurrudin Nagar village of Kanjhawala most of the beneficiaries have telephone, vehicle and other amenities while on the other hand Pundwala Khurd village of Najafgarh have only one telephone. As far as double bed and sofaset are concerned Kanjhawala has first position followed by Mehrauli and Najafgarh block is last because they give perference to cot. In all amenities, Kanjhawala block has first rank. In Qamurrudin Nagar village almost all beneficiaries got better amount of agricultural land. It is clear that higher caste people have more amenities than lower caste as standard of living of upper caste is high. These amenities was considered necessary in upper caste but these are luxurious for poor.

It can be concluded that most amenities are found in high and very high income groups followed by middle and low income group. Total 47 families have telephone and out of this 28 households areof high income group and 15 are of middle income group. Because scooter is not very costly so it was found in all families of various per capita income groups. Eight household, out of eleven who have car belongs to high income group. There is positive co-relation between the per capita income of the beneficiary and the possession of amenities. As the family income increased they realised the need of the above amenities. Radio is replacing by tape recorder. More than eighty per cent households have television and more than sixty per cent have cooler. Higher caste families occupy more amenities rather than lower caste.

Housing Condition

House is the one of the basic requirement for human survival. Housing encourages economic activity, generate employment opportunities and create a basis for healthy and hygienic social life. House is good indicator for economic development.

Table 4.18

Housing Condition of Beneficiaries. (% age of families)

Block	*Double storey*	*Welldecorated*	*Marble*
Alipur	55.0	45.0	40.0
Najafgarh	40.0	27.5	30.0
Kanjhawala	80.0	55.0	55.0
Mehrauli	57.5	52.5	35.0
Shahdara	30.0	40.0	15.0
Rural Delhi	52.5	44.0	35.0

Source: Personal Survey. 154

In the study area double storey houses were commonly found and fourty four per cent houses were decorated by cement, iron, furniture etc. Sabhapur and Biharipur villages have not better housing condition but Ghaorli has because this village got good compensaton money. Like other indicators Kanjhawala block has first position in housing. 80 per cent houses of this block has double storey as Kanjhawala is census town there was lack of space so people build another floor. After kanjhawala, Mehrauli block has good condition of housing as there was more than fifty per cent houses are well decorated and double storey. In lower caste habitation few kutcha houses were found in all villages. Pucca houses were made with cement, brick, iron, furniture etc. Some beneficiaries were using grantite stone on front side of house. Rural houses are now copying the urban design and shape of houses. Rural people realized pridein using urban style. Some rural masses build shop in frontside of house and rooms in back side and on upper floor. Mostly one or two rooms were built on double storey which is commenly used for guest. Differences can be made between higher and lower caste by watching the houses.

Table 4.19
Houses of Different Size of Beneficiaries (% age of families)

Block	*Small size*	*Medium size*	*Large size*
Alipur	25.0	52.5	22.5
Najafgarh	40.0	40.0	20.0
Kanjhawala	22.5	67.5	10.0
Mehrauli	22.5	60.0	17.5
Shahdara	32.5	52.5	15.0
Rural Delhi	28.5	54.5	17.0

Source: Personal Survey

Family has the number of rooms according to his need. According to size, houses have been categorized into three categories i.e. small size house (below 3 rooms), medium size house (4-6 rooms), and large size house (above 6 rooms), In rural Delhi mainly medium size houses can be seen followed by small size. In Najafgarh block 40 per cent houses were of small size and 40 per cent were of medium size. Maximum medium size houses were in Kanjhawala and Mehrauli which has 67.5 and 60 per cent respectively.

For agricultural purposes farmer has to build more rooms for cattle, fodder and storage of food grains, therefore Alipur and Najafgarh block has larger house rather than remaining blocks. Some beneficiaries also made more rooms for rent. When we co-relate the house size to family size, we find that there was close positive co. relation as shown in Table 4.20.

Table 4.20
Family Size and House Size (% age of total)

Size of Family	*Small Size House*	*Mediurri Size House*	*Large Size House*	*Total*
Small	8.0	9.0	2.0	18.0
Medium	16.5	31.5	9.0	58.0
Large	4.0	10.5	6.5	24.0
Total	28.5	54.5	17	100

Source: Personal Survey

Like the house size, small size family has less than 3 members, medium size has 4-6 and large size has more than 6 members in a family. Table 4.19 shows that study area was dominated by medium size families and houses. People have constructed double or multi-storey houses in order to accommodate their family. Four per cent big families have small size houses because they can not afford to built double storey therefore they have to live in 2-3 rooms. On the other hand there were 2 per cent of total sample households have small family but have large size houses.

Table 4.21
Beneficiaries Family Having Kitchen, Bathroom and Toilet
(% Age of Total)

Per capita (annual in Rs.)	*Kitchaen*	*Bathroom*	*Toilet*	*Well decorated*
Less than Rs. 6,000	2.0	1.5	0.8	0
Rs. 6,001 to 15,000	32.0	33.5	27.4	29.5
15,001 to 30,000	43.5	40.0	44.4	44.3
Above 30,000	22.5	25.0	27.4	26.1
Total	100.00	100.00	100.00	100.00

Source: Personal Survey.

Poor family have small house without, kitchen, bathroom and toilet etc. Table 4.21 reveals that family having kitchen, bathroom toilet mainly belongs to high per capita income group and this group constitute largest percentage of total. It can be concluded that as the income increases facilities and amenities is also increase. Before the implementation of programme rural people had mostly kutcha houses and small size houses but now condition is really better.

Energy

The pattern of energy in rural Delhi has undergone a major change under the impact of urbanization, resulting in the reduction of rural areas by 14,800 hectares between 1970 and 1986. While the total cropped areas has fallen to 0.89 lakh hectares in 1983-84, from 1.13 lakh hectares in 1960-61, the area not available for cultivation in the rural belt of Delhi has increased from 0.34 lakh hectares to 0.64 lakh hectares during the same time period, due to agricultural land having been putting Jo non-agricultural and related uses. Agricultural wastes and cow dung have developed market potential and are therefore not available freely to the landless. Collection of fuels in rural areas has by and large become a more time- consuming occupation and a health hazard due to burning of unconventional materials for the sake of energy (Solanki, 1988).

The main source of cooking in rural Delhi is L.P.G., emerging at fast rate and use of dung cake and woods is reducing. This LPG is better from health and environment point of view. For domestic need 56.5 per cent beneficiaries are using it. Maximum user ofcooking gas were recorded in Mehrauli and Kanjhawala block and except Shahdara remaining all four ,blocks have more than fifty per cent consumer. In Shahdara more user were found in Gharoli. Many respondents told that they have applied for gas connection but they are in waiting list. Before the benefits of programmes rural masses collected agricultural waste, wood, dung cake for domestic need but now they are pursuing LPG and kerosene oil. People get kerosene oil from fair price shop. Those living in urban villages have better access to cooking as; Kerosene was main source of energy. Almost in each household of rural area can be seen mud chullah. Newly married bride is bringing cylinder of LPG in dowry. Therefore it can be said that in the area of study, pattern of energy for cooking is changing rapidly. It was pointed out by people that out of the total suffered persons from air borne disease and 63 per cent were using mud chullah as the main source and this chullah emit more smoke. Females generally paid more time to chullah than other member of family. In can be said in brief, that before the implementation of programme socio-economic condition was very bad but at present situation in good and programme has showed its positive response and impact. Among all the five blocks of Rural Delhi more improvement was recorded in the villages of Kanjhawala and Mehrauli block.

Health Condition

Health is very important factor for overall human development. Rural people of Delhi generally have sound health. As they take more pure milk, oxygen.

Table 4.22
Suffered Persons by Different Disease (% age of total)

Block	*% of Total Suffered*	*Airborne disease*	*Waterborne disease*	*Other disease*
Alipur	4.8	33.3	8.3	58.3
Najafgarh	3.9	33.3	22.2	44.4
Kanjhawala	5.7	25.0	16.6	58.3
Mehrauli	5.6	31.0	23.0	46.0
Shahdara	5.1	33.3	8.3	58.3
Rural Delhi	5.06	31.0	17.2	50.8

Source: Personal Survey

The picture that emerges from the primary data relating to the incidence of disease shows that people largely suffered from cancer, anemia, thoirid, accident etc. There were 51 per cent who belonging to this category followed by airborne ind waterborne diseases which accounts 31 and 17 person respectively. Blockwise analysis of the data shows that in all blocks non-communicable disease and accident case accounts for a major share of ill health. Patients of waterborne disease were maximum in Mehrauli and Najafgarh. Villages of Najafgarh block dependence of hand pumps which are shallow and there was possibility of hand pumps water mixing with the underground water. The health condition of masses can also be related to their economic condition.

Table 4.23
Health Conditions of Different Per Capita Income Group
(% age of total)

Per capita Income (annual in Rs.)	*Suffered from Air borne disease*	*Water borne disease*	*other disease*	*Total*
Less than 6,000	5.2	0	3.4	3.5
6001 to 15,000	47.0	44.9	53.3	50.0
15,001 to 30,000	36.8	55.5	43.3	43.0
Above 30,000	10.5	0	0	3.5
Total	32.7	15.7	51.6	100.0

Source: Personal Survey

It can be concluded from analysis of data that maximum suffered persons were found in middle and high income group. Although low income group families have number of patient but either they were not aware or they did not want to tell. Patients of T.B. were largely found followed by asthma it may be due to mud chullah causing indoor air pollution or congested houses Rich families were more aware about their health and they were very careful about their treatment. On the other hand poor people were very careless because of not capable for costly treatment, if they go Government hospital then they have to kill earning time so they were in pitiable situation.

References

Lamba, P. S. & Solanki, S. S. (1988), Science, Technology and Rural Development, Anmol Publication, New Delhi.

Mohammad, N. (1988), Caste and Primary Occupation, Concept Publishing House, New Delhi.

Rao, R. V. (1978), Rural Industrialisation in India, Concept Publishing House, New Delhi.

Solanki, M. S. (1988), Energy and Rural Delhi in Lamba, P.S. & Solanki, S.S. (eds.) *op. cit.*

CHAPTER–5

STATUS OF PEOPLE'S PARTICIPATION AND PERCEPTION

Introduction

For any developmental programme, people matter because it is for their welfare that such programmes are implemented. Generally participation means getting people to agree and to go along with a project which has already been designed for them. According to Julius Nyerere "Rural development is participation of people in a mutual learning experience involving themselves, their local and outside resource. People can develop themselves by participation in decision and cooperatives activities which effect their wellbeing." Participation should include the notions of contributing influencing, sharing or redistribution power and of control resource benefit, knowledge and skills to be gained through beneficiary involvement in decision making. So, Participation is a voluntary process by which people influence or control the decision that effect them. So, the essence of participation in exercising voice and choice and developing the human organisational and management capacity to solve problems as they arise inorder to sustain the improvements. In other words participation should not only stop at information sharing, but decision making and initiating action are important and essential components of participation.

Importance of People's Participation

Popular participation enriches the planning process by checking the reliability of data ensuring commitment of the people to target projects for the rural sector; rationalising proposals by the agencies concerned; reducing unreasonable pressure through informal channels and finally basing the proposals on the judgements of the people affected by the programme (Reddy, 1979). Significance of the participation was felt by the planners, social scientist and administrators etc. The effective rural development strategy must therefore involve the people themselves and their institutions at all levels in the schemes from the formulation to the implementation of the programme. Participation engenders financial, social and psychological costs as well as benefits. Masses are likely to participate when their benefits outweigh their costs. The local communities are in a better position to develop integrated programmes which alone can avoid duplication, minimise delay and ensure easy accountability. As a result of participation the rural folk will be in a better position to assess their own rights and responsibilities.

Local people know their problems better and how and where a facility should be located. They are the best judges of their own interest. Also, as a result of the mass's participation, the beneficiaries can get the maximum from the administrative agencies. Carl C. Taylor based upon his observation of Community Development Programme of

Government of India, has reduced the process to its simplest term. He says there are four steps:

1. The worker must involve the villages in systematic discussion of their felt needs
2. Systematic planning to carry out of the first self-help project selected by the community.
3. Harnessing the resources of community for carrying out a concreate project; and
4. Creation of community appreciation and determination to undertake additional projects (Taylor, 1956).

The Balwant Rai Mehta Committee observed, "Rural development and rural welfare are possible only with local initiative and local direction. In the ultimate analysis, it must be an instrument of expression of local people's will taking in view the local development (Mehta, 1957)

The main objectives of people's participations can be:

(1) Better planning and implementation of rural development programmes.
(2) Mobilisation of additional resources required for programmes
(3) Empowering the people, particularly the poor to play and effective role in rural development.

Extent of Participation

The extent of participation depends on the institutional arrangements, the content of programmes and the spectrum of beneficiary groups to which they appeal. After processing of primary data it was found that only few per cent households were participating in rural development programmes in rural Delhi. But there is large gap in participation between lower and upper castes as more than fifty per cent participants were belongs to higher caste.

Most of the respondent told that they were not aware of any other programme whether any rural development programme is going on or not. They said that if Government launch any programme for rural area then block officials give the information to only village leader and rest of the villagers do not get any information and much of the benefit was consumed by official body with the help of village leader. Respondents express their view furiously that if any villager go to the block office for information then he does not get any correct and reliable information. In spite of giving emphasis on betterment and upliftment of rural masses theachievements is not so satisfactory from target point of view. More benefit has reached to particular section of society rather than common men.

Therefore, ignorance of people on the part of a majority of respondents may be attributed to the fact that officials come to the village to meet the leaders, discuss with them and leave the village. They hardly make any efforts to get acquianted with common men of village. Villagers say that officials come with preconceived notions, programmes and schemes ahead in their bags. They were rarely take trouble to find out the felt needs of the people of rural areas. There were several problems associated with such participation. The major obstacles to popular participation are absence of a strong commitment on the part of the Government; unhelpful attitude of civil servants, lack of awareness among the rural poor, inadequate use of the mass media and rural power structure. The rural population to a great extent differs in economic and social status. Generally the richer sections show an attitude of indifference to programmes meant for the poorer sections. There is saying that twenty persons can drive a horse to the pond but none of them can make it drink. Similarly the Government can put forth its maximum efforts to ensure development of rural areas by way of developmental programmes, augmentation ofresources incentive schemes, but all these efforts do not guarantee maximum return unless the client in development take interest and participation in the development tasks.

Measures to Strengthen People's Participation

People's participation is to be ensured through generation of awareness and the promotion of the motivation. Institutions need to be set-up at the local level through which the poor can express their views on going programmes and these views should receive due attention at higher levels.

The planner should educate the beneficiaries on the benefits that flow from various programmes and the sacrifices involved. Participation should start at the stage of deciding what to do and how to do it.

The following measures may tie taken to mobilise people to join the main stream of development.

A. Measures should be taken to understand the ground dynamics and the heterogeneous character of society. It is necessary to understand how a community views a particular problem.

B. Special attention must be given to identify the resources of the people and to educate them to understand their needs and problems.

C. It would be better if individual and household development plans were drawn up and masses motivated to take active part in their own development.

D. People must realise that the ultimate responsibility of the supporting the programme lies with them only and for which they have to work consistently and collectively towards the mobilisation of the resource and

E. Monitoring should be an inbuilt feature of the programme in order to avoid any undesirable incidents (Bajpai, 1995).

Popular participation should be ensure to voluntary organisations which are closer to the local people. Of course, the nature of the institutional structure, the prevailing value system do influence the nature and extent of people's participation in developments. To give the real shape of the term "participation" with our existing situation for overall development fallowing suggestion has been made by Keenroard Virhagen.

1. First, as a developmental strategy to combat poverty, people's participation must be kept distinct from classical charity and welfare approaches.
2. Secondly participation should start at the stage of deciding what to do and how to do.
3. Thirdly, rural people should be given the opportunity to develop their organisation.
4. Fourthly, every rural organisation should be allowed to proceed at its own pace of development in harmony with its own capacities of self

administration and self organisation but external support must be provided when it is required.

5. Fifthly, people's participation should be an expression of the aspiration of group members to improve and to control the circumstances of their lives (Bhawmick, 1984).

Thus, participation is valuable and indispensable from more than one point of view. People themselves are the assets and the largest beneficiaries of such participation. Ultimately socio-economic development is based on individual and group initiatives.

People's Perception

Opinion, attitude and perception play very important role in getting out the real rural picture. Apart from the villager nobody can describe reality of rural environment. To find out the people's perception in the rural Delhi certain questions were asked from them. Emphasis was given on that what they perceive about socio-economic environment of villages. Participative Rural Appraisal(PRA) technique is also used in research study for genuine and reliable unbiased information. This PRA technique helps us to understand the rural poor and appreciate their perception and their needs. The PRA is defined as a semi-structured process of learning from, with and by rural about rural condition. The PRA is based on certain simple truths:

(1) There is a lot of information available with the local people; about local resources and local problems.

(2) If local people are involved in planning any scheme meant for them, they can come up with useful ideas

and contribute to the success of the planning process and

(3) This would also ensure proper use of the facilities made available to them (Varadan, 1993).

Factors Influencing Rural Inequality

Inequality as a concept is closely related to the term poverty. A higher level of inequality will tend to be associated with a higher level of poverty. Non-agricultural section is more unequal then the agricultural sector. The decree of consumption inequality in rural areas is less than that of inequality in land distribution. The per capita consumption of the non-agricultural class is slightly above the average, although the inequalities within their class are perceptibly larger while the per capita consumption of the agricultural worker is lower than that of the other group of the rural population. There is some improvement in the level of standard of living of the low income group families on account of various poverty alleviation programmes.

The factors affecting rural inequality includes:

1. Ownership control and use of assets such as building, land, means of irrigation etc.
2. Sharing of the gains in rural income which turns to be rich farmers.
3. Access to credit and inputs
4. Some development programmes which benefits the rich man more than the poor.
5. Price rise which aggravate the disparity in terms of per capita consumption between richer and poorer sections of the rural society.

Social Status

To find out the social status of beneficiaries of both time period, i.e. before the programme and after the programme, a scoring scheme has been adopted. Score from 1-5 is represents low status,6-10 shows the medium and more than 10 depict high social status (Table 5.1).

Table 5.1

Scores According to the Social Status

Status	*Scores*
Low	1 -5
Medium	6-10
High	>10

Table 5.2

Social status of beneficiary families (Pre Benefits of pro-gramme) (% age of families)

	High	*Medium*	*Low*
Alipur	27.5	22.5	50.0
Najafgarh	25.0	5.0	70.0
Kanjhawala	12.5	7.5	80.0
Mehrauli	12.5	2.5	85.0
Shahdara	2.5	12.5	85.0
Rural Delhi	16.0	10.0	74.0

After benefits of programme (%age of families)

	High	*Medium*	*Low*
Alipur	32.5	17.0	25.0
Najafgarh	42.5	* 52.5	5.0
Kanjhawala	52.5	37.5	10.0
Mehrauli	40.0	47.5	12.5
Shahdara	80.0	20.0	0.0
Rural Delhi	49.5	40.0	10.5

Source: Personal Survey

Table 5.2 reveals that 3/4 of the beneficiaries had low status in pre benefits of programmes in rural Delhi and in today's life there was found only ten per cent to beneficiaries households who have low social status. Earlier the order of social status categories of beneficiaries was in this way maximum persons were belong of low status followed by high and medium status but at present this order has changed as maximum beneficiaries perceive themselves under high social status followed by medium and low. To get genuine situation author requested to the respondent to tell real condition without bias about their social status. The respondents of the block of Shahdara, Kanjhawala and Mehrauli told that now they are in better in social status as these blocks are more urbanised.

Caste Discrimination

Scheduled castes have suffered from the culture of repression of the caste people for long time. The caste system emerged according to the association of individual with different functions they performed in the society. Earlier there was found neck to neck feeling of casteism but now a days its loosing its tightness.

Table 5.3
Problems of casteism faced (%age of families)

	Before	*After*
Alipur	67.5	12.5
Najafgarh	77.5	50.0
Kanjawala	77.5	35.0
Mehrauli	82.5	17.5
Shahdara	95.0	12.5
Rural Delhi	80.0	25.5

Source: Personal Survey

A close examination the data presented in Table 5.3 shows that in comparison to earlier, people have positive attitude about casteism. More than 3/4 respondent report that they had to face the problem of caste discrimination on each and every step of life 20 years ago, but today 1/4 respondents were suffering to caste discrimination. Maximum suffer persons were recorded in Najafgarh's villages. Few respondents told that high caste people do not allow to enter in the temple of village therefore some times issue related to caste becomes the metter of conflict and tension between higher caste and lower caste people. At the time of allocating surplus land the percentage of suffering families weremore than sixty per cent in each block of rural Delhi. But today social scene of villages were changing as many of the upper caste people have the opinion of non-casteism but on the other hand a few lower and upper caste persons told that this system of casteism will be continued forever and it will not last at all. Auther has also observed the casteism is breaking and new generation is going to against it.

Table 5.4
In favour of casteism (%age of families)

Block	*Before*	*After*
Alipur	57.5	5.0
Najafgarh	52.5	4.0
Kanjawala	15.0	5.0
Mehrauli	12.5	2.5
Shahdara	02.5	0.00
Rural Delhi	28.0	10.0

Source: Personal Survey

Transformation in general denotes the substitution or succession of one thing in place of another. There is no doubt that in all sections of society the feeling of casteism is going to weak but there was also some people who want to retain this system. Ten per cent families havethe attitude in favour of it. The people who have conservative thinking, they told that caste system should not eradicate even few lower caste person are also supporting it. Author noted that interaction of different caste people was increasing and upper caste people also adopting the occupation of lower caste. In brief, it can be said that perception of people about casteism was changing and in future one day this system will end.

Table 5.4 tells about people's thinking and attitude. In comparison to earlier time people's ideology has changed now. 77.5% beneficiaries families believes that success or failure of life depends upon education and hardwork of

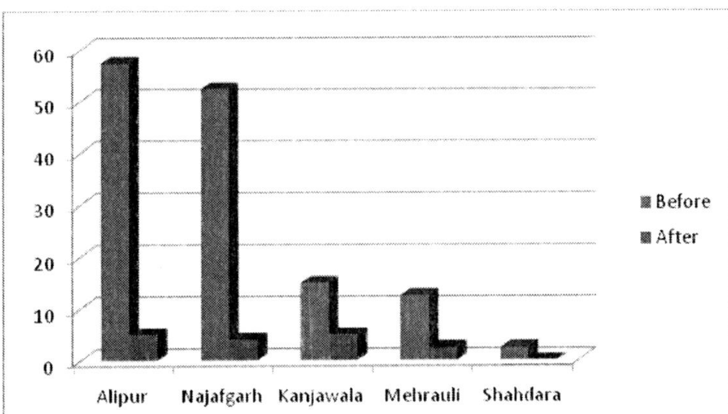

Figure 5.1: In favour of Casteism (%age of Beneficiary Families)

Table 5.5

Success or failure depend upon (%age of total)

Block	*God*	*Education & hard work*
Alipur	20.0	80.0
Najafgarh	35.0	65.0
Kanjhawala	20.0	80.0
Mehrauli	17.5	82.5
Shahdara	20.0	80.5
Rural Delhi	22.5	77.5

Source: Personal Survey

human beings. We can conclude from data that people of Najafgarh block has more conservative thinking, rather than people of other villages.

Table 5.6

Reasons for Not Reaching Full Benefits (%age of total)

Block	*Corruption*	*Middlemen*	*Can't say*
Alipur	45.0	*50.0	05.0
Najafgarh	50.0	47.0	02.5
Kanjhawala	65.0	35.0	00.0
Mehrauli	40.0	47.5	02.5
Shahdara	57.5	42.5	00.0
Rural Delhi	57.5	46.5	2.0

Source: Personal Survey

Respondents reported that benefits of programmes are not reaching to the needy persons due to various reasons, but 57.5 per cent told that corruption was main reason which can be seen in each department from bottom to top. They told that benefits was grasped by whole official body. Government documents show that substantial amount has been spent for rural development but in reality conditions of infrastructure was not good.46.5 per cent people told that role of middlemen was another barrier in the path of taking benefits. They said that for taking loan, middlemen demands 20-25% commission of the total loan. Therefore 98 per cent of the respondent believes that corruption and middlemen consumed biggest percentage of benefit for rural development. Poor persons reported that because upper caste people have link to official body so this group get more benefit.

Table 5.7
Utilisation of increased income of respondent
(% of families)

Block	*Buying Land*	*Business*	*Children's Education*
Alipur	17.5	17.5	65.0
Najafgarh	5.0	17.5	77.5
Kanjhawala	5.0	15.0	80.0
Mehrauli	5.0	20.0	75.0
Shahdara	15.0	17.5	77.0
Rural Delhi	9.5	15.5	75.0

Source: Personal Survey.

3/4 of the respondents said that if their income increase than they will spent it on education of their children. In study area most of the families's first priority was to teach the children both son and daughter. Even a few families want to send their children in public or convent school rather then Government school for better education. 15.5 per cent of respondent stated that first of all they would like to earn money by business. Families which have not enough space for living they want to buy the land for residential and agricultural purposes. In the category of buying the land and business most of them were poor household. Ultimately it can be said that rural people are adopting urban attitude as well as urban life.

Table 5.8
Suggestion for Improvement of Rural Development Programmes (%age of total)

Per Capita Income Group in Rs.	*Programme should be transparent*	*Priority for infra- benefits*	*Direct Representa- tives*	*Structure to needy*	*Total*
Below 6,000	0.00	0.00	5.5	0.00	02.5
6,001-15,000	46.2	33.3	37.7	37.5	38.0
15,001-3,0000	28.5	57.1	45.5	45.0	45.5
Above 3,0000	25.0	9.5	11.1	17.5	14.0
Total	14.0	21.0	45.0	20.0	100.0

Source: Personal Survey

On scruting of the data given in Table 5.7, it was found that on overall basis 45 per cent of the beneficiaries said that benefit of any programme should be given directly without middlemen while 21 per cent wants that programmes should be infrastructure facilities oriented. Some respondent said that only villagers know the rural area's problems so in decision making process one member of villages should be as representative of the rural areas. Official information of any programme was given to the Gram Pradhan or Village leader only and this information does not spread in whole village so 14 per cent of respondents want that this information and programme should be transparent, when we correlate suggestion to income group, we found that high per capita income have given emphasis on infrastructure facilities while lower income group on direct benefits ultimately, it was found that a big percentage of rural population wants corruptionless, accountable and fair administration.

References

Bajpai, P. K. (1995), People's Participations in Development, Mainstream, July, New Delhi.

Bhawmick, P. K. (1984), People's Participations: A Conceptual Reality, Kurukshetra, Vol. 32, No. 17, Govt.of India, Delhi.

Mehta, B. R. (1957), Community Projects and National Extension Service, Vol. I Govt, of India, New Delhi.

Reddy, Y. Venugopal (1979), Multi-Level Planning in India, Vikas Publishing house, New Delhi.

Taylor, C. Carl (1956), A Critical Analysis of India's Community Development Programme, The Community Project Administration, Govt, of India, New Delhi.

Vardan, M. S. S. (1993), An Exercise That Works Wonders. The Hindu, August 29, New Delhi.

CHAPTER–6

SUMMARY AND CONCLUSION

The socio-economic and cultural set-up of society matters enough to assess the development parameters in rural society. The geographical landscape on the one hand and cultural norms of society on the other hand, always govern the developmental phenomena. Development has been described as a generic term meaning growth, evolution, stage of inducement or progress. Rural development can be described as a process aiming at improving the well-being of people living outside the urbanized areas. Rural development is not merely the agricultural development but a rural transformation, which includes development of all the facets of human life. It is to be viewed in its totality rather than a fragmented approach. Realizing the backwardness of the rural area, many ruraldevelopmental programmes were started by the Government for theeradication of rural poverty and to improve their living condition. The first step in this direction was launching of Community Development Programme in October, 1952. The objective was bring on all round socio-economic development of the villages with the co-operation and participation of the villagers. Later on many other programmes were launched form time to time. Despite the implementation of different programmes, still now, many villages of Delhi are suffering from lack of infrastructure facilities. Many of the programmes resulted in failure.

The objectives of the study have been approached through primary and secondary sources of data, but main source of data were from primary household survey. Analytical approaches were supplemented by statistical and cartographic technique to visualize the patterns of change.

The study area consists Rural Delhi, covering total five blocks namely, Alipur, Najafgarh, Kanjhawala, Mehrauli and Shahdara. Out of the total one hundred ninety nine inhabited villages, ten villages (two villages per block) were selected randomly. Among these ten samples villages, Kanjhawal was selected deliberately as this was a census town rather than rural village. To assess the socio-economic condition of rural poor a household survey of beneficiaries of Twenty Point Programme was conducted. The fact behind chosing this programme was that apart from this programmes villagers were not aware of the other programmes.

So, this research study is base^ on evaluation of beneficiaries under this programmes. An interview schedule was prepared keeping in view the objectives of the study for collecting primary data. This interview schedule consisted of five parts viz. personal characteristics of beneficiaries and their families, socio-economic status, health and people's perception and suggestion. Fourty samples of beneficiaries from each block were chosen for primarly data. Secondary data were also collected form different agencies, institutions, reports and journals. The present study has been organised in six chapters but main chapters are fourth and fifth which fulfil the major objectives of research study.

Delhi lying within a narrow strip of the Indo-Gangetic Plain, has long history of its growth during which it saw many rises and falls of the population. It has been ruled by the Hindus, the Muslims and the British in past. Each of the rulers of that period organized and controlled the administration of Delhi in a different way from the others, which affected the functional, areal and population growth of Delhi. Urbanization and industrial development of Delhi necessitied large vacant land. The study reveals that total number of rural villages has decreased from 341 in 1951 to 209 in 1991. No doubt that urban area is encroaching the rural villages at higher rate. Since 1901 to 1991, two decades recorded remarkable increases in population of Rural Delhi, first time in 1941- 51 and second time between 1981-91. Immigration rate is higher than the natural increase. Due to urbanization process the percentage of rural population to the total is continously decreasing.

Villages of Rural Delhi are losing their traditional rural system,but older generation wants to retain it. Rural masses are trying to adopturban life style in each aspect of life. Now rural villages of Delhi are exposure of semi-urban. It were the villages near to the urban area showed a greater degree of the urban influence. In the whole country, Delhi has the highest per capita income and per capita investment in infrastructure development. Because it has more job opportunities, people from other parts of country were migrating and pressure of population on resources were increasing. Land use pattern has changed significantly over the time and at present agriculture land is being used for commercial purposes. As encroachment on agriculture land wasincreasing so agriculture land as well as total rural area was diminshing. Small land holding has increased in numbers and decreased in size while large size holding has gone down in numbers and size.

Present research study took the programmes implemented after 1975 so it covers Farmers Training and Education Scheme, Rural Development Corporation, Land Reforms 20-Point Programme, Small, Marginal and Agricultural Development Agency, Integrated Rural Development Programmes. National Rural Employment Programme, Rural Landless Employment Guarantee Programme, Training for Rural Youth and Self Employment, Development of Women and Children in Rural Area, Jawahar Rozgar Yojna, Development and Construction of Panchayat Ghar, Integrated Rural Energy Programme, Integrated Development of Rural Villages and Rural Water Supply Programme etc. Government records were claimed that significant amount has been spent in various rural development programmes and schemes, but rural masses did not agree to this.

All these programmes had their own aims and objectives. This research work has put emphasis on 20-point programme under which surplus land was distributed to the landless and weaker section of society. Before this programme poor persons were in pitiable condition therefore Late Prime Minister Smt. Indira Gandhi implemented it for the upliftment of weaker section. As per instruction of Government surplus land was distributed among eligible families. Most of the Gram Pradhan distributed it with partiality as they also allotted it to non-eligible families.

In some villages beneficiaries had to struggle more for allotment of land, i.e. Kanjhawala Land Scandal. Most beneficiaries got this land infertile, barren, sandy and very far from their residential place. This programme had notable impact on life of beneficiaries. This land opened the door of self-sufficiency, social justice, prosperity for the family of beneficiaries. But on the other hand some beneficiaries reported that due to this land some problems were created.

Although Government documents indicates that significant amount of money has been spent in rural development sector but villagers were saying that they have not got any benefit apart from Twenty Point Programme. They were telling that amount allocated to rural development sector has gone.in the pocket of officials. The success of any development programme depends as much on the response of those persons for whom it is intended. Only those persons in the villages who have easy access to the block officials were able to get benefit. The Governmentis trying to provide all felt needs in rural areas but growth rate ofpopulation is surpassing the infrastructure facilities. The facilities which are found in urban area of other states, can be seen in rural villages of Delhi, therefore the condition of rural area is better in comparison to other parts of the country.

Area of study is dominated by middle size of houses and families. Houses of lower casts were found in periphery and no where near the centre of village. Some of the activities located in an area were once not approved by the rural society but at present upper caste arebuidling new houses in the vicinity of the lower castes. In society larger people got education upto twelfth class, but still now, one big section of society is illiterate, mainly old age persons. Before the implementation of 20-point programme fifty per cent of working population was land labourers who used to go on the field of Zamindar because at that time "Jazmani" system was more prevailent but at present most are in diversified activities of secondary and tertiary sector. The occupational structure was also undergoing change and as a result of this the economic standards were changing. Relationship between caste and occupation and economic status were weakening. More than eighty per cent respondents belongs to Rs. 6,001-30,000 per capita annual income while 25 years ago mostly were in indigence condition. Families, who took loan for business purpose near about ninty per cent started saving and overall 75 per cent of beneficiaries were able to save some money for future.

Out of the total beneficiary families 37 per cent were doingcultivation and land of remaining families were sold or acquired by Government for community purpose. Mainly agricultural practice is going on in the villages of Najafgarh and Alipur block. There were many reasons to leave this occupation but strong reasons were low economic condition, increasing urbanization and encroachment by the other activities. Because agricultural land is being to used for other purposes total numbers of buffaloes are also decreasing therefore it is clear that economy of Rural Delhi is shifting from primary to other occupations.

Material possession of respondents has increased. Telephone, Car, Refrigerator and Sofa set were found in the houses of high income group. In middle income group families fan, mud chullah and cycle were being replaced by cooler, cooking gas and scooter. Throughout, study area has dominance of double storey houses because of various reasons. In comparison to earlier situation houses are in better condition with modern facilities and of different type of materials.

Among all the five blocks socio-economic status of Kanjhawala and Mehrauli were higher. In whole rural Delhi, villages of Kanjhawala block showed more socio-economic development after the implementation of programme. These blocks are more involved in urban activities. Health profile of people are almost satisfactory. However, various non- communicable diseases are prevalent followed by air borne diseases. Non availability of toilet was the main problem because open space was reducing and the villager did not have the facility of sewer system.

Certainly the changes have beer^ found in the overall life. The generation gap is the major reason. The process of transformation in daily life is a very slow process and the process always parts its impact on the running rural system. As regards to social change we find a change in the attitudes of casteism. The positive values has been expressed more in respect with regard to low caste people, changing traditional caste occuaption, modern fashion etc. Before the benefits of programmes lower caste poeple were discriminated on the basis of caste but today this type of situation was not there. Jointfamily was being replaced by extended family. Still joint family is the dominant feature. Upper caste and lower caste people came closer and were co-operating with each other. This Programme broke the cycle of dependency.

One thing is common in area of study that they were not aware of rural development programmes and schemes. Most of them reported that Government launched many programmes but these programmes do not cross the boundary of B.D.O and information was confined only to village leaders. Therefore the extent of awareness and people's participation was little. Official bodies do not try to enhance awareness and participation of common people. Respondent's main complaint was that Government organizations are full of corruption. Without bribe no benefit could be obtained. Share of benefits of needy persons goes in to wrong hands. 45 per cent respondents suggested that benefits of any programme should be reached directly without any middlemen. Villages are suffering from corrupt administration.

It is clear that Twenty Point Programme had positive impact on life of beneficiaries and socio-economic change and development has been taken place. If weaker section develops then village develops and if villages develops then country develops.

SUGGESTIONS

The study suggests the following suggestions.

1. Most of the rural children get general education and after education they became jobless so one technical subject should be introduced at higher secondary level. For rural poor there should be free education with scholarship upto graduation level.

2. Standard of Government school should be similar to the public school and accountability of teachers about result should be fixed.

3. A survey in each village of poor persons should be made and special programmes must be launched for upliftment of identified people. In these programmes priorities should be given to income generating activities.
4. They should be provided with interest free loan with easy terms and condition to set up small scale industry and preference should be given to younger educated unemployed. Subsidy on agriculture inputs should be given to small and marginal farmers.
5. Adequate assistance should be given directly to needy person. To set up village industry, licence should be strictly provided to villagers only.
6. After implementation of rural development programmes, an evaluation and assessment study should be carried out annually.
7. Information of any programme should be made available to the whole village. The problem of awareness can be tackled effectively,if the programmes are given publicity through means of mass- communication.
8. Programmes should be formulated with discussion with rural people and a rural representative should be a member in the committee. Emphasis should be on enhanced participation of people.
9. Administration should be fair, transparent and accountable and impartial.
10. Basic amenities such as safe drinking water, drainage, medical facilities and sanitation particularly toilet should be simultaneously provided. Infrastructure

facilities should be covered by all sections of society of the village.

11. Each village should have a permanent training centre of different trades for women which will impart skill for income generating activities
12. Each village should have a large Community Hall where people ofwhole village can discuss any issue in order to promote interaction of different people.
13. To impart the innovative ideas, positive attitude, modern thinking there should be one lecture in village once a week for personality developement for both males and females.
14. Reservation in Government jobs and educational institutional should be continued for next ten years. There should be a Mahila Mandalat village level where all women can participate in order to raise their problems and find out their solution.
15. Government should ensure that the beneficiaries should not be made to pay bribe at any stage to derive the benefit. In case of any such report, a thorough investigation should be carried out and defaulting official dealt with strictly.

BIBLIOGRAPHY

Acharya, B.T. (1991), Rural Industrialisation : A Catalyst in Action, Himalaya Publishing House, Mumbai.

Adarash Seva Sangh, Indian Journal Rural India, A.S.S. Mumbai.

Alexander, K.C. (1980), Economics Development and Social Change, Behavioural Science and Rural Development, Vol. 3, NIRD, Hyderabad.

Anker Desmond, L.W. (1973), Rural Development : Problems and Strategies, International Labour Review.

Arora, R.C. (1979), Integrated Rural Development, S.Chand & Sons, New Delhi.

Arora, Ramesh K. (1979), People's Participation in Development,HCM State Institute of Public Administration, Jaipur.

Aziz, Sartaj (1978), Rural Development: Learning from China,the Macmillan Press Ltd. London.

Behari, Bepin. (1976), Rural Industrialisation in India, Vikas Publishing House, New Delhi.

Bhatia, S.S. and Lai, A.C. (1963), Geography of Delhi, Science and Culture, Vol. 20, No. 12.

Bhadouria, P.B.S. and S.C. Dua, (1986), Rural Development Strategy and Perspective, Anmol Publishing, New Delhi.

Bhaduri.Amit. (Ed.) (1982), Studies in Rural Participation, Oxford & IBH Publishing Company, New Delhi.

Bhattacharya, S.N. (1970), Community Development Analysisof the Problem in India, Academic Publisher, Calcutta.

Brahmanda, P R. (1987), Dimension of Rural Development in India, Himalaya Publishing House, Delhi.

Brahmanda, P.R., B.K. Narayana and A. Kalappa (Ed.) (1987), Dimensions of Rural Development, Himalaya Publishing House, Mumbai.

Brunches, Jean (1952), Human Geography, Rand Menally & Co., New York.

Census of India, Primary Census Abstract of Delhi, 1971, 1981,1991, 2001, 2011. New Delhi.

Census of India, District Census Handbook of Delhi, 1971, 1981, 1991, 2001, 2011, New Delhi.

Chaturvedi, T.N. (Ed.) (1986), Rural Development Some Themes and Dimensions, Indian Institute of Public Administration, New Delhi.

Chowdhary, D.Paul. (1978), New Partnership in Rural Development,M.N. Publishers, New Delhi.

Chottopadhyay, D. (1985), Rural Development Planning in India,S. Chand & Sons, New Delhi.

Choudhary, S.N. (1987), Dynamics of Rural Power Structure,Amar Prakashan, Delhi.

Deogaonkar, S.G. (1980), Administration for Rural Development in India, Concept Publishing Company, New Delhi.

Dak, T.M. (Ed.) (1989), Rural Industrialisation Challenge and Perspective, Northern Book Centre, New Delhi.

Danda, Ajit K. (Ed.) (1984), Studies on Rural Development: Experiences and Issues, Inter-India Publication, Delhi.

Delhi Administration (1976), Gazetteer of Delhi, Delhi.

Delhi Administration (1987), Gazetteer of Rural Delhi, Delhi.

Delhi Administration (1995), Bureau of Economic and Statistics for Delhi, Delhi.

Desai, A.R. (1961), Rural India in Transition, Popular Book Depot, Mumbai

Desai, D.K. (1983), Management in Rural Development, Oxford & IBH Publishing Company, New Delhi.

Desai, Vasant. (1988), Rural Development : Programmes and Strategies, Vol-I-V, Himalaya Publishing House, Mumbai.

Dhillion, D.S. (1991), Integrated Rural Development, Vohra Publication and Distributors, Allahabad.

Diwakar, A and Qureshi, M.H. (1996), Utilisation of Compensation Money after Land Acquisition in Rural Delhi, Urban India, Vol.I

Gangrade, K.D. (1970), A Comparative Study of Leadership and Social Structure in three Delhi Villages, Ph.D. Thesis, Department of Sociology, University of Delhi, Delhi

Ghate, Prabhu. (1984), Direct Attacks on Rural Poverty, Concept Publishing Company, New Delhi

Government of India, First of Ninth Five-Year Plans, Planning Commission, New Delhi.

Government of India (1985), Evaluation Report on IRDP, Planning Evaluation Organisation, New Delhi.

Government of Delhi, Delhi Quarterly Digest of Economic and Statistics, Delhi.

Fanshawe, H.C. (1902), Delhi : Past and Present, John Murry, London.

Franda, Marcus. (1970), India's Rural Development, Indiana University Press, London.

Friedmann, John. (1973), Urbanisation, Planning and National Development, Sage Publication Ltd., London.

Indian Institute of Mass Communication.(1980), Rural Development and Communication Policies, I.I.M.C, New Delhi.

Jain, S C. (1983), Impact study of IRDP : Uchchhal Taluk,South Gujrat University.

Kumari, M. Ashok. (1989), Rural Industrialisation in India : A Strategy for Rural Development, Mittal Publication, New Delhi.

Lamba, P.S. and Solanki, S.S. (Ed.) (1988), Science, Techonology and Rural Development, Anmol Publication House, Mumbai.

Lamba, S.K. and J.S. Tomar (1986), Impact of Land Reforms on Rural Development, Agricole Publishing Academy, New Delhi.

Lambert, Richard, D. (1962), The Impact of Urban Society Upon Village Life in Roy Turner (ed.) India's Urban Future, University of California Press.

Lea, David, A.M. (1983), Rural Development and the State,Metheun & Co, Ltd. London.

Madan, G.R. and Madan, Tara (1983), Village Development in India : A sociological Appraoch, Allied Publishers Private Ltd. New Delhi.

Mehta, Shiv R. (1984), Rural* Development Policies and Programmes, Sage Publications, New Delhi.

Ministry of Rural Development and Employment, Indian Journals, Kurukshetra and Gramin Vikas, New Delhi.

Mishra, R.P. (1985), Rural Development: Capitalist and Socialist Paths, Concept Publishing Company, Delhi.

Nangia, Sudesh Kumari (1972), Patterns of Rural Settlements in Delhi Region, Ph. D. Thesis, Department of Geography, University of Delhi, Delhi.

National Institute of Rural Development, Indian Journal of Rural Development, NIRD, Hyderabad.

Pawar, S.N. and Patil R.B. (1994), Problems and Prospects of Development, Cooperation, Voluntaryism, Communication, Social Tensions and Weaker Sections in Rural India, Mittal Publications, New Delhi.

Ramchandraiah, G. (1986), Impact of IRDP and NREP in U.P. : A study, Kurukshetra, Vol.36.

Rao, D.R. (1988), Rural Development Issues, Ess Ess Publications, New Delhi.

Rao, D. Vasudeva (1985), Facets of Rural Development in India, Ashish Publishing House, New Delhi.

Reddy , V.K. (1988), Rural Development in India : Poverty and Development, Himalaya Publishing House, Mumbai.

Ratnam, V. Nittala & Rao, Bhaskdra B. (1982), The Management of Social Development in Rural Areas, Newman Group of Publishers, New Delhi.

Sau, Sachinandan (1988), Rural Development : Theories and Experiences, Allied Publiser Limited, New Delhi

Saxena, D.P. (1994), Rural Towns and Socio-Economic Development of Villages, Mittal Publications, New Delhi.

Schwarzweller, Harry, K. (1995), Research in Rural Sociology and Development, Jai Press Inc. London Vol. I-VI

Shah, D.R. (Ed.) (1989), Alternative in Rural Development,Sterling Publishers, New Delhi,

Sharda, Ram Dev (1977), Status Attainment in Rural India,Ajanta Publications, Delhi.

Shuman, Michael (1974), Towards a Global Village, Pluto Press, London.

Shrivastava, V.K. (1983), The Indian Journal of Marketing Geography, the Association of Marketing Geographers of India, University of Gorakhpur.

Singer, Milton (ed.) (1975), Traditional India : Structure and Change, Rawat Publication, Jaipur.

Singh, K.N. & Singh, D.N. (Ed.) (1985), Rural Development inIndia, National Geographical Society of India, Varanasi.

Singh, K.S. (1996) People of India: Delhi Anthropological survey of India an Mandal, Vol, XX.

Singh, Kanwar Jasbir (1982), A Study of the Socio-economic impact of IRDP on different sections of rural population in Punjab, Ph.D. Thesis, Punjab Agricultural University, Ludhiana.

Singh, R.B. (1986), Geography of Rural Development, Inter- India Publications, New Delhi.

Singh, Surender (1984), Some Aspects of House Types and Housing Problems in Rural Delhi, Ph.D. Thesis, Department of Geography, University of Delhi, Delhi.

Srinivas, M.N. (1978), India's Village, Media Promoters and Publishers, Mumbai

Thingalaya, N.K. (Ed.) (1986), Rural India-Real India, Himalaya Publishing House, Mumbai.

Todaro, Michael P. (1956), Economics of Developing World,Longman Group Ltd. London.

Training Orientation and Research Centre (1994), Study of Assets of Rural Delhi, Department of Social Work, University of Delhi, Delhi.

Tyagi, V.K. (1982), Urban Growth and Urban Villages, Kalyani Publishers, New Delhi.

Unnithan, T.K.N. (1956), Gandhi and Social Change, Rawat Publication, Jaipur.

UNRISD (1970), Contents and Measurement of Socio-Economic Development, Geneva.

United Nations (1989), The Socio-Economic Impact of Rural Development Programmes on Low Income Groups,

Economic and Social Commission for Asia and Pacific, New Delhi.

Verma, Ram K. (1996), Country Experiences in Rural Development. Printwell, Jaipur

Varshney, A. (1995), Democracy, Development and the Countryside, Cambridge University Press.

Wiser, Willaim, H. (1958), The Hindu Jajmani System, Lucknow Publishing House, Lucknow.